Critical Guides to French Texts

4 Corneille: Horace

Critical Guides to French Texts

EDITED BY ROGER LITTLE, WOLFGANG VAN EMDEN,
DAVID WILLIAMS

CORNEILLE

Horace

R. C. Knight

Emeritus Professor of French
University College of Swansea

Grant & Cutler Ltd
1981

© Grant & Cutler Ltd
1981
ISBN 0 7293 0094 3

*Hmm
PQ
1754
K64
1981*

I.S.B.N. 84-499-4525-9

DEPÓSITO LEGAL: V. 817 - 1981

Printed in Spain by
Artes Gráficas Soler, S. A. - Olivereta, 28 - Valencia (18)
for
GRANT & CUTLER LTD
11 BUCKINGHAM STREET, LONDON, W.C.2.

Contents

Horace, the First Classical Tragedy

IN seventeenth-century France, Roman history was studied in schools (as French history was not), and figures from Roman history were much quoted in moral or political treatises. The story of the three Roman brothers who fought to the death with three brothers from nearby Alba to end the war between their cities was therefore common knowledge before Corneille used it in this play. He was not even the first French playwright to use the theme, though the earlier plays are now forgotten.

The tale is in Livy, a Roman historian, and Dionysius of Halicarnassus, a Greek historian, both working in the age of Augustus (Bibliography, *9, 10*). Both these accounts deserve to be read. Livy tells how Roman and Alban troops were about to join battle when their leaders called a truce and agreed that three champions from each side should fight it out. He stresses the fierce patriotic feeling among the watching soldiers; and tells for the first time the well-known story of how one Horatius was left alive on the Roman side, unwounded, to face three Curiatii, and cleverly turned and ran, thus separating his opponents who were more or less severely wounded, so that he could dispatch them in turn. He adds — it seems almost like a postscript — that on his way home Horatius met a sister of his, mourning for one of the Curiatii to whom she happened to be betrothed; she had recognised among the spoils of war a cloak she had woven for him. Horatius killed her, was tried for the grave crime of fratricide, and was eventually acquitted by the Roman people.

We shall see that Corneille does not find room for the pathetic detail of the cloak; but that he sees far better than Livy did what can be made out of the fact that there must have been friendship, and there was going to be a relationship through marriage between these two teams who had been killing each other, and between their families.

Dionysius, in his own way, does give emphasis to this. In the first place, he says both sets of brothers were triplets, and sons of two twin sisters who had married on the same day and given birth on the same day; in fact, the cousins had grown up as one family. In the second place, he makes much of the patriotic fervour with which they accepted their task as a great honour as soon as it was offered to them — the Curiatii jumped at it at once (more eagerly than Corneille's Curiace), the Horatii only asked leave to consult their father, who approved and praised them.

I have begun with Corneille's sources because they show us what materials he had in front of him when he decided to make the story into a play. It would be a great mistake to think that using a source shows lack of originality. All plots come from somewhere; nobody invents stories 'out of his head' — if they do not come from books, they come from experience; the author's, or somebody else's. The most the author can do is to mix, to change, or rearrange, to choose where he will lay the emphasis or what he will omit. The most important insight we can get from knowing a writer's source comes probably from seeing the points at which he is not satisfied with it, breaks off, and deliberately makes a change — and from trying to guess why. Such changes are signs of the quality of his own taste and imagination.

Corneille put his play on in 1640, first in a private performance for his patron, then at the Théâtre du Marais, one of the two permanent public playhouses in Paris. It was by far the more recently constructed, and had identified itself with modern tendencies in drama and literature.

The nub of the original story — the fight, the ruse of Horatius, and his unexpected victory — were things he just could not show. Even had he wished, he could not have set up a sword duel of six men, watched by two armies, on his stage which had some twenty-four feet of clear space between the wings by less than thirty feet deep.[1] But to him, as a playwright, the subject offered another conflict, one that he could exploit; a conflict of loyalties and duties — not between the Alban and the Roman camps, but inside each character involved, between the family ties and the patriotism, which are both emphasised in the sources. Corneille was a seasoned playwright already, with ten plays behind him. They had mostly been successful, but the play before *Horace, Le Cid,* had been a sensational triumph, and there already he had drawn all his effects from just this kind of moral conflict; the central characters in it are a couple passionately in love, and separated by a vendetta based on a code of honour in which they both passionately believe. Patriotism was a theme with a deeper and more universal appeal than vendetta.

Horace is then a play where a Roman family, closely linked with an Alban one (we shall see that Corneille strengthens the links he found in his story), faces an almost intolerable conflict of loyalties. It contains moments of excitement and suspense, but more importantly it is a study of the moral conflict — not, however, a static abstract analysis but a developing action where each character in turn comes forward to speak of his dilemma and explain the decision he makes. Each point of view is treated sympathetically by Corneille, and claims our sympathy.

So it ought to be a moving play. It is; its moments of climax are thrilling. But it would be very surprising if that were the first reaction of any reader (English- or even French-speaking) who came unprepared to it today.

What does he find? He finds nothing, I am afraid, except a series of speeches, some very long, in verse and in a rather difficult French, which must strike him as archaic and stiff. Anything that is *done* is done off-stage. 'Action' here does not mean the preparations for a battle or the deaths of five of the six men who fight the duel. We shall see later what happens

---

[1] J. Lough (*28*, p. 61) says roughly 42 feet, but he appears to include the row of dressing-rooms behind the stage.

about the one killing (in IV.5) which could have been shown on the stage, and is not. Notions of the dignity of tragedy (*la bienséance* in one of its applications), and no doubt also the difficulty of portraying violence convincingly with the means at their disposal (an aspect of *la vraisemblance*), were beginning to stop all that, just at the time when *Horace* was produced (see below, p. 43). When I refer to the 'action' of *Horace* I shall mean, as do all other critics, principally the progressive shifts that take place in the relations between the characters, because of what they do, or simply what they say.

If our reader could imagine or see the play as it was produced in Corneille's time, I am not sure that he would be much helped. Not that elaborate stage devices had not been invented, or scenery providing an illusion of great distances by the skilful use of perspective — but that was not in France, but in Italy, where wealthy patrons in several cities were making drama, and principally opera, an occasion for profuse and gorgeous display. Paris had neither the playhouses nor the resources to imitate this (though two Italian operas were brought in later, in private theatres, by the Italian minister, Mazarin). At the time of *Horace* things were going the other way: serious tragedy was beginning to avoid using even such stage machinery as there was, and to do without changes of place from scene to scene, which could only be indicated by having 'flats' representing the different localities all on the stage together side by side, [2] or else hiding the back of the stage with 'tabs' that could be drawn temporarily across, having a new scene painted on them. There may have been a front curtain, but it was never used to hide the whole stage for scene changes, as it is today — it was apparently too cumbrous to move quickly enough.

---

[2] Consult pl. 40-53, pp. 80-81 of T. E. Lawrenson, *The French Stage in the Seventeenth Century* (Manchester U. P., 1957) but note that only pl. 48 shows the decor of a tragedy, the *Pirame et Thisbé* of very early date, probably 1621; or *Album Théâtre classique: La Vie théâtrale sous Louis XIII et Louis XIV,* iconographie réunie et commentée par Sylvie Chevalley (Paris: Gallimard, 1976), pp. 12-17.

Horace is, in fact, the earliest tragedy we know which observed 'Unity of Place' in the strict sense which later became universal — the stage shows the same room in the house of the Horaces from beginning to end of the play. French theorists of the theatre — who were much listened to in this time of great changes in dramatic form and style — had read Aristotle's *Poetics* and misapplied his frequent statements that events in a play should take place 'in accordance with probability' (*vraisemblance* was the French translation) 'or necessity'. They made *vraisemblance* forbid all changes of scene because they thought they disturbed illusion. We know that they do not, because Shakespeare has proved it; but seventeenth-century Paris did not know Shakespeare.

But even so, do we go to see *Hamlet* principally to see a ghost, a scene on the ramparts and another in a graveyard, a fencing-bout, and four corpses at the end (none of which Corneille would have allowed, though he had indulged in such things ten years before, in *Clitandre,* his first tragicomedy)? I think we go mostly to hear Hamlet's soliloquies. And it was on his speeches that Corneille was depending by the time he wrote *Horace* — dialogues more often than soliloquies; the rest of what comes into a tragedy is optional extras, which his period decided to discard. Literature, including drama, is an art in which it is the words that remain; while a play that depends on spectacle risks being forgotten at the end of its run.

In fact, Samuel Beckett in our day has used experimental forms of drama where the stage is much barer and more neutral than Corneille's was. The production at the Théâtre du Marais must have been highly conventional in the sense that it showed what would be accepted as an early Roman house, but by no means an attempt to reproduce the architecture or costume of that period, for no one knew (or thought) anything about historical accuracy. Not an empty stage, but one containing no objects specially connected with the play, except when Horace brings in three swords in the fourth Act. Formed of painted canvas 'flats' arranged to form wings and a backcloth, it might well have been used before, or would be used later for other plays. It would probably be more ornate than we might think appropriate (for on painted canvas, marble, bronze, and gilding cost no more than plaster), and the architecture would be that of a fine mansion or palace of the early seventeenth century. This is simply guesswork founded on the only evidence we have — frontispieces of the printed plays of the time (such as can be seen in the Chevalley album mentioned in note 2) — but I know of no such illustration showing the interior of a private dwelling, used in a tragedy, anywhere near the date of *Horace*. Besides, we can never be sure the artist is not using his imagination; and in any case he quite naturally chose to illustrate, when there was one, the scene of exciting physical action that the playwright could not represent. That of *Horace* shows the hero's victory in the duel.

Horace and Curiace, coming from the wars, would probably wear great cloaks, with helmets, cuirasses, and Roman military kilts such as we can see in innumerable statues, medals, and historical paintings of the seventeenth and even eighteenth centuries. We see them in the frontispiece of the play, which has often been reproduced. [3] The other actors probably wore costumes of the seventeenth century, rendered more theatrical with an abundance of plumes, and false jewellery for the women. The only movement to catch the eye would have been of speakers 'sawing the air' in gestures and poses we rightly call theatrical. They all spoke, apparently, with a heightened and rather artificial declamation, but probably moved little on the stage. The illustrations we have show them grouped downstage, usually facing the audience, where the lighting (hanging candelabra and possibly footlights), and audibility, were best. Their acting consisted in speaking; the words carried the message; the words were the play.

But the words themselves provide the last obstacle, for they are in a style unfamiliar enough to make any modern reader coming to them for the first time quite unable to

---

[3] Or perhaps not helmets; for such eighteenth-century reminiscences as we have speak unanimously of plumed hats (see J. Lough, *28*, pp. 72-73).

believe that they moved the seventeenth-century public to enthusiasm.

It is not a case of unfamiliar words, nor simply of words with unfamiliar meanings or in unfamiliar constructions — though there are some of them, and it is necessary to know, for instance, that *déplaisir* (lines 11, 1459) [4] is close in meaning to *ennui* (205), both implying grief; that *soudain* (74, 77, 1321) means 'at once', and *lâchement* (496) 'without moral firmness'; also that in *il lui faut applaudir* (21), *tu me viens de réduire* (673), *lui* and *me* must be understood with the infinitive, not with the first verb.

But the real difficulty is closely connected with the appeal to the mind, rather than the senses, which we have just discussed in relation to play production. Language is used here, not as it is most often today (in French or English), to narrate events or depict people or scenes, but almost entirely to describe what cannot be *pictured* at all — situations or problems which may involve some dilemma where choice is difficult, and characters, responding to their situation with their minds and emotions, facing their dilemmas and making their choices. These are the occasions when men and women are most truly themselves, so Corneille clearly feels, and most worth watching. (We may compare the idea of 'existential choice' which Sartre has made familiar.) For the seventeenth century, it followed that in language the vocabulary of ideas and conceptions, abstract and generalized, was more 'elevated', nobler, than the concrete and particular. Nouns and verbs connected with more ordinary departments of life seemed 'bas et vulgaires', and were avoided in serious writing. 'Homère est exact à décrire les moindres particularités: ce qui a bonne grâce dans le grec' wrote Racine in 1662, annotating the description in the *Odyssey* of Odysseus making a raft. 'Notre

---

[4] All editions of the play have the same numbering. My quotations are from the first edition (1641), as reproduced by W. G. Moore and P. H. Nurse (Bibliography, *1* and *3*). It rarely differs from the definitive text of 1682, and I shall discuss any significant changes affecting the lines I quote.

langue ... fuit extrêmement de s'abaisser aux particularités, parce que les oreilles sont délicates et ne peuvent souffrir qu'on nomme des choses basses dans un discours sérieux.' If a spade had to be referred to, it was better to call it an agricultural implement, because this at least explained it by assigning it to its proper genus and species among objects. If Corneille refers to hands, arms, feet, hearts, or weapons, it is by metonymy, i.e., in order to speak of something done to, or by, the possessor of these things. Thus, to open *Horace* at the beginning, in lines 8-10 the words *larmes, soupirs, yeux,* speak of weeping but refer less to the physical act (which in fact Sabine, the speaker, is *not* performing) than to her emotions, of which tears would be the natural sign. We find too in this passage that the workings of the inner man (or woman) are reasonably, if somewhat unexpectedly, departmentalized; dismay belongs to *le courage* (= *le cœur*) (4), strength of mind *(la vertu)* to *l'esprit* (5), grief to *l'âme* (11).

This first speech of Sabine's needs to be read with all these points in mind. (And I ask my reader to read it before, or while, he reads my commentary.) It may look like a sterile argument on an absurdly trivial question ('May I cry?'), based on very frigid psychological analysis. It is in reality the important 'scène d'exposition', in which the playwright has to tell us what we need to know if we are to follow the action. These facts (about the war between Rome and Alba) are placed in the mouth of a character deeply affected by them, who can interest us by making us feel and share her grief and apprehension. But, as we should expect from him, these emotions are not the subject of a lyrical effusion (for which they might well seem appropriate): they form an argument, in which our moral judgement will also become involved, and it is only for the sake of the argument that the speakers mention their emotions at all.

Sabine's *confidente* has obviously already made a remark blaming her demeanour. Sabine begins by an appeal *(Approuvez ...)* which introduces her defence; her *faiblesse* (which consists of feeling *douleur* and letting it be seen), though to Julie it seems shameful (17), is justified by the circumstances (2). Threatened by *de tels orages* (the only metaphor in the speech and, typically, a fairly conventional one, even *les plus fermes courages* (4), *l'esprit le plus mâle* (5), may yield, but only thus far (11), without disgrace (*sied bien,* 4) — how much more a woman (12, 14)! Of course the unexplained reference to coming disaster is meant to whet our curiosity at the same time as it calls for sympathy. Not only, then, does Sabine judge her emotions as she describes them, but she sketches out a syllogism to prove her contention (which is set out in 1-2). Major premiss (first assertion, 3-6): not even the strongest could avoid some *ébranlement* or *désordre* (this she does not attempt to prove but, characteristically, asserts as obvious). Minor (second assertion, 7-10): she has stopped short of actual tears. Conclusion (11-14): she has not done badly — and she is only a woman. Not only logical neatness but a neat distribution into sections of equal length — two lines (introduction) followed by three sets of four.

A short digression here about this four-line module of which, with some variation and overlapping, of course, the fabric of the alexandrine verse of *Horace* is composed. The reason for the number four seems to me to be a technical one — where lines go in rhyming couplets, and couplets go in pairs, masculine rhymes alternating with feminine, it is I hope obvious that if a poet wants to add or cut anything, he can only do it in a group of four lines or a multiple of four (because less or more would break the sequence of rhymes); so what more natural than to get into the habit of composing in fours? All Corneille's contemporaries do it; the habit is particularly noticeable in Molière — *Tartuffe* 319 ff. and 351 ff. are good examples, where it may well be that Molière thought at different times of different forceful ways of expressing an important (though simple) point, and just stuck them in as successive quatrains. In Sabine's first speech we saw the group of four cut into two equal sentences which roughly repeat each other, but never quite; the second half always adds or changes something; in 15-18 they contrast with each other. One also finds 3 + 1 (49-52), 1 + 1 + 2 (135-38). Julie's reply has 10 lines, in which it seems best to group the first four and the last four together.

Sabine goes on to explain (25-28, 4 lines) why her affections are divided and, with more feeling (three apostrophes, 29, 30, 33, a poetic image, 29; *cher pays, amour,* 30), lays out this time the ties that bind her to each side (*Albe,* 4 lines; *Rome,* 6 lines more freely organized). But, calm or emotional, the verse never loses one formal feature — balance of terms corresponding to the balance of ideas, quite often between words occupying the stressed positions at the ends of two halves ("hemistichs") of a line — either parallel ideas (1, 5) or contrary, forming the favourite figure of antithesis (12, 32). There may be two pairs of contrasted terms (36, 80, 82). The same sorts of emphasis and liveliness can be obtained by other kinds of patterned language; Sabine's third speech (69-94) is well worth studying for this: *Tant qu'* ... *Tant qu'* ...; *Si* ... *Soudain* ..., *Et si* ... *Soudain* ...; *Mais* (the hinge of the whole speech) *aujourd'hui qu'il faut que* ... *Qu'* ... *ou que* ... *Et qu'* ...; *Si* ... *Et si* ...; three lines beginning with *Je* ...; leading up to the two energetic antithetical lines which sum up the sense of the whole speech (92, 94).

It will not be necessary to go on counting lines and labelling figures of speech; but it is well to be able to notice these effects and to realize that they are the basis of that impression of square-cut solidity which we cannot fail to get from Corneille's style.

To recapitulate this chapter, the argumentative first scene of *Horace* is more than an argument — under the logical form we find a sympathetic character in a state of emotion, a threat of dire events to come which arouses curiosity and desire to see the outcome, and a personal problem (caused by a national crisis) which is turned into a moral dilemma with the widest possible relevance (since any of us might have to choose at some time between personal ties and public duty — and here is where the absence of particular detail helps, by diminishing the differences between that situation and ours), and appealing to fundamental conceptions of right and wrong. Later scenes will be found to be similarly based on analysis and debate;

they appear as milestones, periodical opportunities to display the situation at the point it has reached in the form of a balance-sheet of hopes and fears, or the misfortunes of A and B, etc. Another speech of Sabine's, a monologue, surveys her position when the conflict has become a duel where her husband and brother must fight to the death (III.1); she will argue with her sister-in-law Camille, who tries to prove that she, betrothed and not yet married, has the harder lot (III.4). And, of course, the story Corneille took from Roman history forced him to turn most of his fifth act into a murder trial.

Compared with the tirades of lamentation or invective which had seemed the most obvious ingredients of tragedy before his time, these debates are a great advance in liveliness, and often in intellectual depth. Corneille clearly revels in them; he was a lawyer by profession.

Our next step will be to look in some detail at these problems of conduct which he discovered in the historical situation he used, or which he invented and inserted into it. Here, too, there are serious possible misconceptions which may destroy pleasure.

But before going on, a recommendation. I hope that by now I have obliged readers to read quite carefully a large part of Act I, scene 1. Before they can usefully advance further, it is essential, if they have not done it already, that they should read the whole of the play for themselves, however laboriously, with however many misinterpretations (which I hope may be removed later). In the rest of my book I want not to impose my own contentions and quote the text to support them, but to rely on enough knowledge of that text on the reader's part to enable him to challenge, before accepting — or rejecting — the interpretations he will find here. If he rejects, he will not necessarily be wrong, unless there is some real misunderstanding. After that reading, I ask him to keep his copy of *Horace* open at his elbow.

2

The Cornelian Hero

THE French tragedies of the sixteenth century had shown principally heroes that were passive, aware of being helpless in the hands of the Gods, or Fate, or Fortune. In those of Corneille and his contemporaries, characters act or try to act, as I have pointed out, and try to shape their own destinies. [1] The difference is pronounced in *Horace,* which in this respect resembles *Le Cid* far more than it resembles the seventeenth-century tragedies that preceded it. And subsequent tragedies, by Corneille and by others, resemble *Horace* more than they resemble those others. It was for this reason that I called our play a 'classical tragedy', which has come to be the stock phrase for tragedy in the time of Corneille and his rival and successor Racine. It can be called the first classical tragedy in spite of its predecessors from 1634 to 1640.

And yet in Act I of our play we do seem to be still among passive victims who 'just stand there'. These are women characters who, as such, are not called on to fight or to make decisions. But even this appearance is deceptive. Sabine does not lament; she masters her tears. She and Camille do not so much plead when they meet the men in Act II, as argue, bitterly, and fill the last half of the act with their attempts to break

---

[1] The history of tragedy in France, from its beginning in the mid-sixteenth century as a new Greco-Roman form imported in imitation of experiments already begun in Italy, is found in some form in many editions of *Horace* and all histories of French literature. The sketchy outline to be found in Appendix I on p. 70 may however be useful by enabling me to stress the points which will be important for my discussion of *Horace,* and giving the reader something to turn to whenever he feels the need. More names and dates will be found in the Chronological Sketch, p. 73.

down their resolve. When they fail, it is true they cannot then do anything more to affect the fate they have to suffer — until Camille joins the gentlemen, so to speak, and turns her last speech into an act that obtains her the death she desires.

But it is the men, the younger Horace and Curiace, who receive the limelight. What they do does indeed still arouse the 'pity and fear' that Aristotle looked for in tragedy (see p. 58), but something else too — what Corneille later on calls admiration.

Their predicament is unexampled: close friends, they are chosen to fight each other to the death as champions of their respective countries. Their decision — Horace's decision rather, for Curiace is there to make a contrast —, especially the style and spirit in which it is made, is equally remarkable. Above all, it is exciting and uplifting, because it is unexpected.

This is a point which must be made emphatically. If we say, 'Here we have a Noble Roman, who is going to demonstrate for us how one should meet the demands of patriotism'; if we say, 'Horace is a Cornelian hero, so of course whatever the cost he will put his duty first without hesitation', we have killed the play stone dead. We know he is a fine soldier and much respected. But we do not know whether he can take *this* fence, the highest he has ever been put to. Then he does it, in a style and with words that take our breath. As the friend, Curiace, says:

> Je vous connais . . .
> Mais cette âpre vertu ne m'était pas connue. (503)

This is to anticipate. We must look in detail at the situation in which he finds himself through no fault of his own, the dilemma it poses, and the choice he makes.

At the end of Act I a truce had been declared between the city-states of Rome and Alba. Supremacy was to be decided, not by a battle, but by a fight between three champions on each side. Act II is to begin with the announcement of the choice of champions: they will be the three brothers of each of the families we already know, linked by friendship, by the mar-

riage of the Roman Horace to the Alban Sabine, and by the
love of Curiace and Camille, now awaiting their wedding the
following day (337 ff.). Knowing how to make the most of his
material, Corneille arranges it so that the news of one choice
comes before that of the other.

Horace has just heard, in II.1, that he and his brothers are
chosen. His friend makes the suitable comments, congratulating
him, but with reservations; because, as he says (and not wholly
out of desire to please, I believe), the news bodes ill for his own
city (363-70). Horace modestly thinks, or says he thinks, that
Rome could have chosen better (371-76); but — and here he
shows neither boastfulness nor modesty: a brave or noble man
in Corneille's day felt no duty to depreciate his own virtues —
he will die rather than betray his cause, and in that spirit he
does not despair (377-88). Curiace is already dwelling on the
dark side — either his friend must die, or his own city must
lose her freedom (again, 389-97); Horace dwells on the *gloire*
(400, cf. already 378) that he will gain even if he dies (398-402).

Now (sc. 2) the second and heavier blow falls. Curiace and
his brothers have been picked by their city. The two friends on
the stage will have to fight one another. Curiace speaks first,
since the news is brought to him. His reception is what we
should expect (417) — though he has no thought of drawing
back (418-20) — and left alone with his friend, he rails against
their fate: or rather, not against Fate, or the Gods whom he
does not think of as responsible, simply against this grim coincidence. (For we must not misunderstand lines 423-30: they
mean, 'let heaven, hell, and earth do their worst (= even if they
do), it cannot be worse than this; I challenge them to try'.)

Horace faces the crisis differently; perhaps Curiace has given
him time to adjust, but by temperament he sees things differently. What he says now demands the most careful attention.
'Our uncommon misfortune is really an uncommon honour,
because *le sort* is showing how highly it esteems us.' *Le sort*
need mean no more than 'our lot', 'the lot we have drawn', in
other words 'chance'; but it looks as if, perhaps because it suits
his argument, Horace is hinting at the hidden hand of some
God or destiny. In any case, it is only another way of putting a

not inappropriate reflexion — 'weaker men would break under this; all the more credit to us if we don't.'

He goes on to show why it is so uncommon a misfortune: 'mourir pour le pays' any man can do, and should do gladly because of the honour it brings (437-42); they are serving their countries when it means attacking their nearest and dearest (443-48), a thing so painful and difficult that, despite the honour, very few would wish to take it on.

Curiace is one of those who would not, though he will, since he must — with horror and repulsion (474-75) and even self-pity, but no hesitation.

So Horace makes his position clearer, blunter, more brutal. To be a Roman (483) is to be without weakness (486): not only is he resolute (490), because this duty is so exalted that it cancels all lesser obligations (497), he is glad, because of the *gloire* that is inextricably mingled with it. He will fight the brother as happily as he married the sister (499-50), for Curiace is the champion of Alba, and no longer a friend but an opponent (502).

This is the speech which has earned Horace such a bad name (this, and of course even more the murder that the same cast of mind makes him commit in Act IV; but that comes later, and his attitude here, which Corneille has taken such pains to portray, is worth examining by itself — for lines 502-3 are among the most striking he ever wrote).

There are readers who say Horace is an egotistical maniac, who does not care what suffering he causes to others if only he can gain glory.

There is a little truth in that last estimate; while he is not indifferent to the feelings of Curiace (and all the remarks of the first speech of the two include him: the pronoun is 'nous'), he does not, apparently, think at this moment of what their fight will cost the women dear to both of them. I think we must say that the more immediate horror of having himself to fight his friend fills his mind — and I suggest that this is natural and that pain, physical or moral, can make any of us egotistic while it is acute. It is not certain that Curiace thinks of Camille or Sabine either.

Another view is that Horace is some kind of philosopher, either a stoic in complete control of his emotions as Sabine had tried to be (and a Christianised stoicism was in considerable favour in the first half of the seventeenth century — see Jacques Maurens, *20*), or else a man who believed, as Descartes had not yet written, but was about to write, in his *Traité des passions* (1649), that the ideal character was the *magnanime* whose will was in complete control of his acts and, in its turn, was completely controlled by his reason. This was the formula made popular by Gustave Lanson (*11*, p. 95), but now abandoned.

We can push this interpretation further — as Curiace does, as part of his own shocked reaction (480 ff.) — and see Horace as having convinced himself that personal considerations and even human values weigh nothing in comparison with that abstraction *la patrie;* in other words, that an ancient Roman was the image of a modern fascist. Critics of today who are less unsympathetic (e.g. *4*, xvi-xvii) go at least as far as to say he has 'no regrets'; but it is surely right to remember that it is he who spells out — before Curiace, and more poignantly — just what this duty is going to cost them both:

> ... Vouloir au public immoler *ce qu'on aime,*
> S'attacher au combat contre *un autre soi-même,*
> Attaquer un parti qui prend pour défenseur
> *Le frère d'une femme et l'amant d'une sœur,*
> Et *rompant tous ces nœuds* s'armer pour la patrie
> Conter *un sang qu'on voudrait racheter de sa vie* ...
>
> (443)

A juster and more attractive idea of this character has been offered by Louis Herland (*22*, or see a summary in *3*, pp. 40-43). As he sees him, Horace is the more human, fundamentally the more sensitive, certainly the more admirable of the two friends, free from Curiace's self-pity, but valuing their friendship enormously, hoping to be able to rely on it to face their common ordeal, offering his heroic view of that ordeal as help and encouragement to Curiace. Every statement in that first speech (431 ff.) refers to 'nous': if they are united in their way of facing this terrible duty — tremendously honourable, for both equally, because so terrible — they can forget that it is going to end with one killing the other. But then, says Herland, Curiace fails the test and fails Horace, insisting on dwelling on the pain and loss, and asserting not only that the 'honour' is 'fumée', not worth having (459-60), but that his friend is a barbarian (456), inhuman (480-02). Only after that, in angry disappointment at losing the support of his friend and opponent, and perhaps even his friendship, does Horace answer back, urging Curiace to put a better face on it and, in fact, condemning his conduct, though still with restraint (483-84, 487-88), and ending by exaggerating his own stand, even parodying it, saying what in a cooler mood he could not have said and cannot mean. He says in this second speech one thing that is quite true, or at least essential to his way of facing the crisis — that there must be no looking back (488), no entertaining of other considerations (495-96): to do what he has to do, he has deliberately put on blinkers. But he says more, and he says too much: he claims not to 'frémir' at all (490); whatever his country commands, he must perform without question; he accepts not only 'aveuglément' but 'avec joie' (492); and it is right not only to disregard but to suppress ('étouffer', 494) every other sentiment, every other tie (497). Finally he says in a statement one would call hysterical in anyone else:

> Avec une allégresse aussi pleine et sincère
> Que j'épousai la sœur, je combattrai le frère.   (499-500)

And in what is a rhetorical climax, but also the closure of a debate which has become intolerable:

> ... Pour trancher enfin ces discours superflus,
> Albe vous a nommé, je ne vous connais plus.   (501-02)

That last splendid line not only sums up a point of view which we must understand — and must partially identify ourselves with in order to experience the rest of the play with sympathy —; it also shouts to Curiace to go away, because they have ceased to be friends.

There is much that is valuable in this way of reading the
scene. The better we can see that Horace suffers more than he
says he does, the better we can see him as the hero of a
tragedy. The more seriously we take the idea that his blinkered
view is assumed by deliberate choice, his amputation of his
emotional self a voluntary mutilation (cf. Harold C. Ault, *30*),
the more we shall comprehend his inability, later, even to see
any rightness in his sister's opposite extremism, and see how
after his patriotic triumph in Act II, his fratricide in Act IV

Vient de la même épée et part du même bras,   (1741)

and that this is the tragedy of Horace.

It is helpful here to remember what Aristotle says in
his *Poetics,* that the only proper situation for a tragedy is when
a friend — not an enemy or a stranger — is preparing to kill
his friend (chap. 14). Corneille drives the point home in 1660
when he remarks that Horace and Curiace 'ne seraient point à
plaindre s'ils n'étaient point amis et beaux-frères' (*8,* p. 38,
or *6,* p. 833; read the whole paragraph).

One must record a few hesitations over this interpretation
by Herland. He claims to read Horace so deeply that he can
tell when he is saying the opposite of what he means (e.g. in
499), and this is always dangerous, though not unacceptable
out of hand: Corneille is capable of making his characters do
that, and we shall see an example in Sabine. I think I accept
almost all Herland's interpretation, now, on this point. But his
case also demands that we should see Curiace as a decidedly
second-rate personality, who cracks under the test and whose
failure shows up Horace's victory. I do not think this is Corneille's method. We have seen in more peaceful scenes how
Corneille loves contrast and debate and counts on them as an
element in his drama: but you do not improve debate by giving
one side a weak representative; the contrast between good and
bad is obvious, and therefore ineffective; the most exciting
contrast is between two goods, when you cannot have them
both.

The seventeenth century, and particularly the 'enlightened' and sentimental eighteenth century, valued Curiace's retort:

Je vous connais encore, et c'est ce qui me tue,

even more highly than Horace's exclamation — as showing real human sentiments which expose the falsity, or crudity, or one-sidedness of the others. For Herland, the opposite is true: for him, Curiace's belittling of Horace's painful single-mindedness and the ironies which follow ('cette âpre vertu', 'au plus haut point' — an echo of Horace, 489 —, 'que je l'admire et ne l'imite point'), show his pettiness and unworthiness.

The truth is surely that both the antithetical lines are great — one more heroic, one more tragic —, both contain human truth, and their clash is something greater than either. To put Horace's monstrous and heroic stand in its best light, Corneille needed the contrast, not of cowardice, but of an equal and opposite virtue. This is always his practice; many critics have noted the impartiality (to call it that: it is really dramatic sense) with which, like a good professional advocate, he makes the strongest possible case for each of his 'clients'.

A contemporary critic gave a most striking picture of the effect constantly produced on the audiences of his time by

> ces belles contestations qu'il a mises tant de fois sur notre théâtre, qui poussaient l'esprit de l'homme à bout; et où le dernier qui parlait semblait avoir tant de raison, que l'on ne croyait pas qu'il fût possible de repartir; et où les réponses et les répliques excitaient de si grands applaudissements, que l'on avait toujours le déplaisir d'en perdre une bonne partie; et qui contraignaient tout le monde de retourner plusieurs fois au même spectacle pour en recevoir toujours quelque nouvelle satisfaction. [2]

Curiace is right in his way. His pose shows him in a less flamboyant light; but he is voicing the claims of closer and

---

[2] D'Aubignac, *Deux Dissertations concernant le poème dramatique*, 1663. Quoted in my edition of *Nicomède* (London: U. L. P., 1960), p. 24.

more personal human ties, which perhaps it is not imperative to pass over for the big impersonal ones, and surely not to *étouffer*. He is and remains brave, loyal and self-sacrificing. He has perhaps a more complex and (if it is legitimate to imagine him in real life) more attractive character, and more intelligence than his friend. He does his duty, he will pay, and does pay, the price of his divided mind. And if we want a further excuse for him, we might remember that he has just arranged to marry Camille, tomorrow, after two years' separation. The love-interest has been brought right into the middle of the tragic situation here.

As for Horace, there is no doubt that the Romans of the imperial period believed their ancestors to have been very much like this — austere, brave, rough, resolute, fanatically patriotic. This is how the historian Dionysius comments on Horatius killing his sister: 'So averse to baseness and so stern were the manners and the thoughts of the Romans of that day and, to compare them with the actions and lives of those of our age, so cruel and harsh and so little removed from the savagery of wild beasts, that the father, upon being informed of this terrible calamity, far from resenting it, looked upon it as a glorius and becoming action.' (*10*, III, xxi, p. 85).

It is obviously important in judging our hero not to miss the point — by which I mean fly off on a misconception, based on a word we have wrongly taken in a modern sense, or a failure to give proper weight to something that was important in his scale of values. To understand a play of ideas like *Horace,* and react sympathetically to it, we need to form two judgements — one while we are reading the text, the other later, when we ask ourselves whether it has added anything to our own thought.

First, for the few hours we spend reading the text, it is vital to put aside our own ethical (or political) principles, so that we can enter into the fictitious world presented to us and do everything to understand the principles that are being applied there; for only in proportion as we can see their situations in their way can we understand what the characters say and do, experiencing what their creator invented for us to experience. In Corneille's *Le Cid* we have to see a trivial insult like a slap in the face as an outrage which a man of honour can only wipe out in blood; or rather, we have to think in more general terms which we can still accept (and Corneille's vocabulary and style help us to do this), replacing the slap with 'a stain on the family honour', and the death of the person responsible with 'restoring that honour at whatever cost'. In other plays of his, we have to believe that a throne is so valuable that it must always be won if possible, and must be clung to at the cost of death. It is not a question of being convinced in our reason, only in our imagination. Later on, it is only right to apply our own principles; we cannot judge the work fully unless we do.

How do we attempt to understand the principles and systems of ideas on which a work depends, so that we can feel ourselves a part of that world? Above all, by noting carefully what the characters say (as we have been trying to do in this study): they explain themselves far more clearly than people in real life, since there is an author composing their speeches for them. It is necessary to be watchful, miss nothing, and misinterpret nothing; the last is a matter of knowing how expressions may have changed their meanings, and here we can expect commentators to help us. If, when we have done all this, their words and actions seem to make good sense, without inconsistencies, we have some right to think we have succeeded; we shall even have a certain right to look sceptically at the much cleverer systems of explanation that critics sometimes think up, if they ever come into conflict with what we have read in the text. (One such is Serge Doubrovsky: see my remarks in the bibliography, no. *19*.)

Another school of criticism likes to point us to events of the author's time, or ideas prevalent then, telling us that these 'explain' his work, which we shall never 'understand' without knowing them. We are likely to find that this claim means principally that the critic claims to know how certain ingredients got into the work in question (which is a huge claim in any case), but leaves us a long way from 'understanding' those ingredients in any more important sense of the word.

The historical background in 1640, and certain resemblances in it to points in *Horace,* are beyond dispute.

France had declared war on Spain in 1635. (Spain was a long-standing rival, and a much more powerful state, holding the Low Countries to the north as well as the whole peninsula beyond the Pyrenees.) There had been public alarm in 1636 when Spanish troops reached the Somme before being repulsed at Corbie. There were links that crossed national frontiers — the disaffected French nobility used Spain as a natural and convenient ally; the king's wife was a Spanish infanta, whose continued correspondence with her home country had caused national indignation.

The king's minister Richelieu resisted with energy and harshness, and tried to promote a national spirit of what we might call totalitarian devotion to the needs of the country in peril; and being sincerely interested in literature and the arts — and especially the drama — used his patronage to encourage writing along those lines. Corneille was one of Richelieu's protégés from 1635. *Horace* was first played in the minister's private theatre, and the text dedicated to him. Corneille appears proud of having responded to his patron's views, and calls attention to 'ce changement visible qu'on remarque en mes ouvrages depuis que j'ai l'honneur d'être à Votre Eminence', attributing it to the 'grandes idées qu'elle [= Votre Eminence] m'inspire, quand elle daigne souffrir que je lui rende mes devoirs' *(Epître).*

It looks like a clear case; the critics Antoine Adam *(24,* I, pp. 215 ff., 524 ff.), Georges Couton *(13,* pp. 34, 54, 60 ff.), and Jacques Maurens *(20,* p. 198 ff.) make much of these facts. But just what do they tell us about the play?

That as an intelligent and public-spirited Frenchman, Corneille responded to a wave of patriotic concern? — No doubt. That he was glad to note points of resemblance to his Roman story? — Probably; though no one can say the resemblances were particularly close. That this was what made him choose his story of patriotism and sacrifice in the first place? — That we could never prove. (His next tragedy dealt with another kind of national crisis where other parallels have been noted;

but the next again dealt with the martyrdom of a Christian convert — scarcely a topical subject — though the Spanish war was still on, and Richelieu still paying Corneille's annual 'pension' as he wrote it.)

Authors' dedications always made the most they could of the influence the patron had exerted — thus flattering the patron in one way, and the author in another. Corneille made *Horace* look as much like a piece of Richelieu propaganda as he could, *après coup* — that we can believe. He must have been quite delighted at the chance of hearing a real statesman talking about real concerns of state. There does seem to be a certain Richelieu aura about the play, and the two that followed it during Richelieu's life: they are universally acclaimed as Corneille's three greatest, and the contrast is enormous with the first to follow the minister's death, *La Mort de Pompée* (1643). All the fire and conviction has gone out of the would-be heroes, and the interest has shifted to the calculations of a base king and his wicked counsellors.

Two arguments are sufficient to show that *Horace* was not mainly a propaganda piece. The first is that (as we have seen), although Horace's view of country and duty has connections with Richelieu's, it is not the only view in the play; it cannot be said to be better treated than other different views, and there is nothing to say it was Corneille's, or that he intended to recommend it — apart from a few words in that dedication. The second is that if *Horace* had been written to preach a point of view, it would have lost all interest, except for historians, as soon as it ceased to be topical. If it still interests, it is in virtue of its own characters and situations, and the imagination and sympathy with which they are presented. If the reader can make good sense of these without too much attention to Richelieu and the Spanish war, then he may very well judge that the latter are something less than essential to his understanding.

When Horace speaks of 'combattre pour le salut de tous' (437), 'mourir pour le pays' (441), 'servir son pays' (495), a country which has over him 'un droit saint et sacré' (497), his language is readily enough understandable; and Corneille's use

of very general terms makes it impossible to deny the claims
of a duty presented thus in the abstract, as an absolute moral
priority — unless, that is, it seems surprising to us, as it apparently did to a candidate whose script I once marked, that
'in those days it was the custom to put duty before inclination'.
We may want to bring up questions of conscientious objection
or pacifism (which were not of Corneille's time); we may wish
Horace had asked whether the cause of Alba was any less just
than the cause of Rome. We shall have to remind ourselves
that 'My country, right or wrong,' was a respectable sentiment
as late as 1914, and hang on to that.

Unfortunately, Horace uses another set of words almost as
often, which appear to muddle our ideas and call his motives
once more into question. He refers to *honneur* or *gloire*. I
cannot find, as some do, that there is any distinction between
these two terms as Corneille uses them; or only this: that
honour — the English words differ in the same way — comes
from others, and is given, paid, 'rendu' to someone, while
glory is strictly an emanation that radiates from someone, and
that others see and recognise.

Long explanations have been given of what has been
called *l'éthique de la gloire* (see Paul Bénichou, *17,* Octave
Nadal, *18*). It was, we are told, a vestigial remnant in the early
seventeenth century of the feudal lord's pride in asserting his
virtual autonomy, acknowledging only the duty of being true
to himself and worthy of his high station. In Corneille, according to Nadal (*18,* p. 294), 'le devoir ne consiste pas en
definitive à être juste, bon, honnête, mais à satisfaire la gloire,
principe même de l'obligation ou du devoir.' It was the highest
value in life for *le généreux,* the man inspired (by his birth
and breeding) with lofty principles. At its lowest, *la gloire* can
be translated as prestige, and consists simply in being successful, victorious, titled, or powerful, and so being admired; but
it exists on a much higher moral plane, and really noble
natures speak of it as being gained by virtue and not necessarily connected with recognition at all. I think these notions
have been treated too much as if they were closed and mysterious systems shared between initiates. In one form or

another, the thirst for fame must be as old and as widespread as humanity. We saw one form of it in Dionysius of Halicarnassus. Achilles in the *Iliad* chose fame rather than length of days. It was much discussed in Corneille's time, attacked by some moralists as contrary to Christian humility, approved by others as at least a useful stimulus to public service. It should help us to notice that our English culture had the same ideal (see Hotspur and Falstaff in *King Henry IV, part I*), and our vocabulary still contains similar traces — honour, fame, reputation, good name (though not glory, except in the form vainglory; which may be a part of our difficulty with Corneille). Today we call an action honourable, or praiseworthy, without thinking consciously about reputation; neither does a character in Corneille, like Pauline, who neither wishes nor expects her temptation and her victory over it to be publicly known at all (*Polyeucte*, 540, 550).

I suggest that when Horace talks alternately, and apparently indifferently, about duty and honour or glory, he means the same thing: that he has a strong sense of what has to be done — not that he ever attempts to discuss first principles, certainly not with his wife when she attacks them. But as a well-meaning, simple man, he expects to keep a quiet conscience, and — why not? — the admiration and respect of his fellows, as a confirmation that he has done well, and a recompense, the only one he asks, for doing it. His language is more flamboyant than this, as was the manner of Corneille's time (and genre); but this is the essential of what he means.

If anyone had asked him, 'Do you prefer your honour to your wife's happiness?', he might have answered, 'Yes, and so should she; it is my family's honour, and she belongs to my family.' If anyone had asked, 'Do you prefer your country's interests to your wife's happiness?', he could have answered in the same way, 'It is her country too'. And the questions and answers would have been the same question and answer.

He is a heroic figure against a grim background; a kind of tidemark of what human 'vertu' may, in an extreme case, attain: less an example we should all be able to follow, than a stirring ideal — until he has accomplished his task. Then he enters another situation which develops out of the first, and has no chance, no time, perhaps no inclination, to adjust his outlook. He kills his sister; and perhaps he, as well as she, can be called, not now heroic, but tragic.

A last word in justice before leaving the heroic Horace of the first part of the play. His last words in II.3 are much calmer again: three lines of mild irony reply to the irony of Curiace; then he goes to his wife to make sure she sees the consequences for her of his Roman attitude of impersonal rigour in performance of duty. His sister comes in, and he spells it out to her. Either Sabine's brother and Camille's lover will be killed, or Horace himself, and the survivor will have the dead· man's blood on his hands. The dead must be forgotten — he means there must be no recrimination, no thought of vengeance, whichever survives; and he thinks of both possibilities. It is a doctrine that will prove too hard for either woman (cf. Sabine:

> Pourrai-je entre vous deux régler alors mon âme,
> Satisfaire au devoir et de sœur et de femme,
> Embrasser le vainqueur en pleurant le vaincu?   (651))

but it is the right and worthy corollary of the 'vertu' of Horace.

3

Symmetry in *Horace*

THE antitheses in individual speeches, the debates between opposing points of view, and the contrast we have found in the characters of Horace and Curiace, are only a few of the symmetrical groupings which give this play its geometric shapeliness and its tension. (Cf. P. J. Yarrow, *4,* pp. xxviii, 97). The sources in Roman history (cf. above, pp. 7-8 ff.) already provided a balanced situation in which two cities confronted each other, each represented in the final combat by the three brothers of a single family.

One of Corneille's tasks was to prune even this simple pattern — six champions were too many for a stage play; four of them could have nothing to do except say 'Me too' and align themselves behind their spokesmen, their profiles forming parallel lines repeating his, like the opposing battalions in *images d'Epinal.* (And what about their names? They were all Horaces or Curiaces, with different *praenomina,* of which we know only two: *le vieil Horace* was Publius, the victorious son was Manlius. Compare the awkwardness of 'son époux', 995, 'votre gendre', 1115. Camille and Sabine are invented names.) For these reasons they are kept offstage, and as far as possible, out of mind; for it spoils the scene between Horace and Curiace to remember that the fight could have taken place in such a way that they did not have to fight each other at all, one or both being killed by a different brother in the opposing team. It was obvious which two Corneille had to use — the Curiace who loved a sister of the Horaces, and the Horace who was to kill him and kill her.

Two brothers, and a sister (who is in the history too), make three. Corneille invents a fourth to complete a symmetrical pattern and add a different relationship; he will add

one principal character in most of his tragedies after *Horace*.
What is surprising when one comes to think of it, is that
though the couple of lovers was a modern innovation in French
tragedy, never at all prominent before *Horace,* it happens to
have been the couple provided by history; whereas the married
couple, needed for contrast, had to be completed by a co-opted
member. Four front-line characters prove a convenient number for most French tragedies; Corneille often introduces a
fifth almost as prominent; Racine once, but once only (in
Bérénice, 1670), made do with three.

The use of the four in *Horace* is as studied and patterned
as a square-dance. Curiace and Camille have been parted ever
since their betrothal two years ago, and hope to marry the
next day. Horace and Sabine have been married nearly two
and a half years — they would have had time to start a family
if Corneille had not preferred to limit his material (114, 169-
70; 'quelque cinq ou six mois' has been changed in later
editions, probably as being too trivial).

The two Albans (unlike the Alban brothers in Dionysius),
have an antithetical pattern built into their minds; they see
both sides of every question; they understand loyalty to the
state, but could never be totalitarian; they value at least
equally the personal ties of affection and kinship in which men
are individuals. The sister makes the first speech in the play,
and is the first allowed to elicit our sympathy. The brother is
the warrior whose dismay and reluctance we recognise as
being the nearest to our own feelings, however much Horace
may fire our imagination (if he does, as he should).

Curiace, however, is a man and a soldier; he is expected
to act, and this necessity saves him from irresolution, which
he himself would think dishonourable. His principles and
priorities are no different from his friend's, however different
his emotions may be. Not only does he go to the combat, after
battling pathetically with the pathetic pleas of Camille (II.5),
but he echoes in her presence the very statements of her
brother Horace ('Avant que d'être à vous, je suis à mon pays',
562), and ends by paraphrasing the 'Je ne vous connais plus',

breaking off their engagement in an only too obvious pretence that his love is dead ('Je n'ai plus d'yeux pour vous', 590).

His sister, in the first act, had no action whatever that she could take; she saw that she must lose, whoever won. With the return of the men, followed by the arrangements for the combat, she sees a possibility of doing something by trying to dissuade them both. She might have saved her pains, as perhaps she realises; but as a very intelligent woman, she neither pleads nor argues, she tries to shame them by irony. Irony is a weapon Corneille loves, and uses in many ways: readers of texts in a foreign language have some reason to fear it, and even some critics have failed to understand this scene (II.6). So it must be studied closely.

She comes with her husband, who has broken the news to her (see 511-14), to where her brother has just been fighting off the pleas of Camille; and she begins in a fittingly solemn tone of reassurance and approval. Then she comes out with the mysterious announcement of a plan of her own, to remove the guilt (of fratricide) from their action and make them 'ennemis légitimes' (624). The plan is simple, and preposterous:

Qu'un de vous deux me tue, et que l'autre me venge.   (631)

It is reasonable, she says, because once she is dead they are not related (625); and also (a more sophistical reason still) because one of them (but not the other) will then have a just cause (633-34). Does she expect to be stabbed on the spot? Of course not. Why does she propose it? There are deep emotional reasons, which come out later (647 ff.). At the moment what appears is a pretence of taking their fine patriotic principles one stage further. It is splendid to kill your nearest and dearest, honourable because difficult, difficult because horrible; but you haven't gone far enough, and one more killing will make everything right. Now we see retrospectively what irony there was in 'ces grands cœurs' (616), 'digne d'un tel époux et digne d'un tel frère' (620), 'un coup si noble' (621).

How will they react to this *reductio ad absurdum*? Obviously, they are dumb, taken aback, but unconvinced ('Mais

quoi?', 635). She goes on, with an interpretation of their
reluctance which makes their attitude look even worse — their
glory depends so much on horror that it must not be made
less horrible (635-39). So she is ready with a different argument (a Cornelian character will always fight with the best
weapon that is to hand, even if it is clearly a bad one). She
means much to both of them, as wife or sister; so, as they are
bent on hurting and destroying one another, let them strike
at one another through her, and make the sacrifice truly *digne*
(644)! And in fact (final argument, different again), she *is* the
enemy of both (646).

The desperate attempt at bluff and ridicule does not even
receive an answer. She turns to plainer language — why won't
you kill me, since you have made my life intolerable? How
can you expect me to

> Satisfaire au devoir et de sœur et de femme,
> Embrasser le vainqueur en pleurant le vaincu?   (652)

(which was precisely what Horace had told her to be prepared
to do).

She nearly wins (663-66); her husband has to beg her not
to take advantage of his emotion. His father comes to lend
his support, and the only fruit of Sabine's initiative is that
Horace takes note of her threat to appear on the field of
combat (660-62), and has both women shut up in the house
(695-700). He, at this moment, is talking only of honour to
be gained or lost (701-02).

Sabine does lose a little of our sympathy when she brings
out the same demand or challenge twice more in the course
of the action — once when faced with the necessity she
foresaw, to 'embrasser le vainqueur en pleurant le vaincu'
(1383-90); once, before the king, when Horace's life is at
stake, in a new and highly artificial argument that her death
will be the best penalty for his offence (1595 ff.). But in that
scene her later plea at least rings true:

Sire, voyez l'excès de mes tristes ennuis
Et l'effroyable état où mes jours sont réduits:
Quelle horreur d'embrasser un homme dont l'épée
De toute ma famille a la trame coupée!
Et quelle impiété de haïr un époux
Pour avoir bien servi les siens, l'Etat et vous!   (1613)

Trust her always to see both sides! Poor Sabine, everybody thinks the kindest thing to do is to take no notice; and perhaps, given their principles, they are right. Her sufferings are not the least of those we see in this play; she does not make good her threat (654) to kill herself, and the dénouement brings no resolution of her dilemma. Her brother and Camille (one in each family) have ended theirs in death, as we expect to find in a tragedy. But her husband, the other survivor, ends no more happily.

The Roman pair are the single-minded ones. Horace seems to blinker himself by deliberate choice; but Camille does it without hesitation or reasoning — although not all at once. They are single-minded but not simple-minded. Horace does not forget the ties he sacrifices; Camille would be *Romaine* like her brothers if it did not cost too much. She has the conventional sentiment, not exactly patriotic, that she could not marry a man she had to hate as her country's conqueror (144), or else despise as its 'slave' (232). But she represents the commonplace creed of the novels of Corneille's day, that nothing can or must prevail over love; and it is instructive to see that in this heroic atmosphere she is generally condemned.

Act I, sc. 2 leaves no doubt that she is deeply in love: Curiace is her 'plus unique bien' (141). When he suddenly appears (I. 3), she praises him because she thinks he has deserted, just before a battle, for her sake (244-50). She would like to hear him contradict the English poet and say, 'I could not love thee, dear, so much, / Loved I not honour *less*'.

Their second (and last) meeting is full of emotion. Each calls the other 'ma chère âme' (533, 571) (in the first edition: Corneille felt he had to withdraw the expression later as being too familiar for tragedy). Camille uses the familiar 'tu' throughout, as she had done in I. 3.[1]

She tries to argue against his desire for glory (as if that were all, 533, 545 ff.), then against patriotism (563-64). It would not be just to say that she cannot understand his replies, for we do not know: she cannot allow herself to show that she does, for her task is to persuade her lover.

Next, she is exposed to the long suspense (Act III) while the fight takes place out of her sight, and ours. She reacts to the death of her brothers (1009), and joins Sabine in pleading for leniency to the one survivor who is believed to have fled the field (1061). She still believes for a time that her Curiace is still alive and without Roman blood on his hands (1218). Then she has to face first the true report, then the raptures of her father (1141-48), then his lecture (IV. 3) — meant as a kindly exhortation to reasonable and virtuous conduct, but to her intolerable: she has to hear him belittle her loss and tell her to behave as the worthy sister of the man that has killed her lover.

Before the scene which makes the third great climax of the play, in which brother and sister, equally wholehearted, equally strong-willed, meet in head-on collision, we see her nursing her grievances and working herself up to the attack (IV. 4). All this, of course, is contrary to received notions not

---

[1] In both these respects Horace shows a freedom which will not last much longer in French tragic dialogue. Even the use of proper names, except for *confidents,* practically disappears before 1650, leaving a choice between 'ma sœr', etc., 'Prince', 'Princesse', 'Reine' (where appropriate; showing some intimacy or familiarity), and the almost universal 'Seigneur', 'Madame' — which do not appear at all in *Horace.*
Similarly 'tu', after *Cinna,* will be reserved for use to inferiors, or to show great emotion, but normally only by a women to a man. (It is always used in apostrophes, cf. 33, 558). Here Camille uses it to Curiace throughout, except in one line (343) when she is content and serene. He replies with 'vous'. Horace and Sabine *se tutoient* throughout. Horace *tutoie* Camille in Act IV (because he finds her weeping, no doubt) but not earlier (cf. 515): she falls into 'tu' only for her last two speeches. Flavian is *tutoyé* (II. 2), not Julie, who, though a *confidente,* is called a 'dame romaine' in the *Dramatis Personae.*

only of Roman, but of womanly conduct. Her 'impitoyable'
father is a tyrant (1197, 1201). Far from stifling her grief, she
is going deliberately to inflame her own emotions (1201-02);
and she recapitulates at great length (1203 ff.) the vicissitudes
of hope and fear she has experienced, before the final news is
brought — to make it more bitter — by Curiace's rejected
rival, who thinks he has new hope (1225-30). So, if she has
to rejoice and praise Horace in order to be *généreuse* like
him, she would rather be the opposite and 'degenerate' (the
play on words, 1239, is intentional; 'généreux' appears twice,
in the line before and the line after). As she sees him approach,
she determines to provoke him, by an open display of the
grief he had forbidden (1246-48). Is she consciously courting
death? It may be not; for nobody afterwards thinks Horace
ought to have killed her. But there may be a great deal in the
intuition that Sabine will express, that she got what she
wanted, and is to be envied (1381).

As for Horace's feelings, as he runs into her straight after
leaving the scene of his horrible and glorious victory, those
we shall never know for certain; and if Corneille realised this,
he must have regretted it bitterly, considering the care he has
bestowed on presenting the sister's emotions and intentions.
The fault, for it surely is one, has been forced on the playwright by his dramatic technique. We may quite well imagine
that the returning champion may have exchanged at least a
few words with his soldier-attendant Procule, which we might
have been allowed to hear, and thereby have gained some
notion of his present feelings — though it is by no means easy
to imagine what they would have been, least of all in that
cup-tie atmosphere. It may be that Corneille — like the Roman
historians — felt there would have been too much public
jubilation for the hero to be himself, even for a moment. But
such a conversation could have balanced Camille's monologue
and given us some understanding of what happens next: only,
where could Corneille have fitted it into his play?

The difficulty about 'unity of place' is slight; it was still
quite ordinary to hide the back of the stage by a curtain drawn
across for certain scenes, and possibly painted to represent a

street (as for the open-air scenes in *Le Cid,* I. 3-6, II. 2, III. 5-6). But what about the order of the scenes? If a Horace-Procule scene had preceded our present IV. 1, it would have revealed the outcome of the fight and spoilt the effect of surprise as we learn it at the same time as *le vieil Horace* from the lips of Valère. And who would have told the story? — either Horace, who would have to be shown glorying in the deaths he had inflicted, at greater length than now (1251-56), or Procule, an obscure ranker (and no doubt an inferior actor, since he has such a small part), telling Horace what he knew already; and Corneille was very sensitive to this kind of consideration, as his *Examens* and *Discours* of the 1660 edition show. After IV. 1, there is no vacant space, the action is continuous [2] — Valère finds Camille and her father on stage (sc. 2), the father admonishes her before he leaves (sc. 3), and leaves her raging (sc. 4). She must not be left to cool off before the fateful encounter. The author could have managed differently and given Horace a monologue as he comes in — but at the price of taking away Camille's. One of them had to go without.

So we must read the scene of the meeting carefully to pick up what clues there are.

---

[2] A scene in a French play begins and ends whenever an actor (except very minor ones) enters or goes out; nothing else happens to mark the fact, certainly not a curtain — a front curtain, even when present, never falls between acts in the seventeenth century. When in a play like *Le Cid* the supposed place changed from one scene to the next, it was obvious that no actor in the first could remain in the next, and the empty stage became a signal of the change; when there was no such change of place, at least one actor always stayed on stage (or at least, before going, saw or heard, or was seen or heard by someone coming in). This 'liaison de scènes' becomes a way of assuring the audience that the place is still the same; or, when this is no longer necessary (because of the strict Unity of Place), that the act is not yet over. The convention became a rule. So 'Exit Camille. Enter Horace', as English printers would have put it, is impossible. Camille could have left after saying 'Il vient' (1249); but she was in no mood to do anything of the sort.

Horace certainly blusters in like a parody of himself, his three soldiers (reduced to one in later editions) carrying the swords of the dead Curiaces. He brandishes 'ce bras' (his own of course, named three times, 1251-53), talking of vengeance, 'ma gloire' and 'ma victoire'. His own triumph and that of Rome seem to bulk about equally in his eyes. We see that he uses *tutoiement* as he had not before.

Deliberately, Camille speaks of her tears (no doubt she is weeping), and her brother seems obtuse in thinking they are only for the dead brothers, as in his book they ought to be. Or is he unwilling to think or seem to think that she has someone else in mind?

They are avenged, he says. After repeating this in what must be ironical tones (1262-64), Camille goes on with her programme, naming first 'un amant', then 'mon cher Curiace', and dares to call for vengeance for *him*. Horace, indignant (or is there something else?), calls this criminal (1271) and shaming (1274), and will only speak of his defeated enemy as the Alban whom he 'no longer knew' (502), 'un ennemi public', to be forgotten (cf. 530). His last words ('mes trophées') sound absurdly egotistic: I think they are a vivid way of repeating that she must dwell on national good fortune, not on private loss.

For this she calls him 'barbare' (1278), 'tigre' (1287), utters the forbidden name again, dwells on her loss which is all she can think of now (1284 ff.), and calls down misfortune on him, especially what to him is the greatest of misfortunes, the loss of that cherished glory of his (does she see or hope for what is coming?). Her brother's reply is very violent (as shown by the language — an exclamation, a rhetorical question, the repeated imperative 'aime', words like 'rage' (= madness), 'mortel'): she has disgraced their family, and he cannot permit it (1297). As for the attack on himself, perhaps the word 'outrage' refers to it, but no other; and when he is finally stung into action, it will be on behalf of Rome, not himself.

But now Camille seizes on the name of her real enemy, Rome, in a rhetorical,[3] violent, even hysterical outbreak. It is made to sound like unconscious, or inspired, prophecy — a device which was fairly common in the fifth acts of tragedies of this time, for the purpose of extending the twenty-four hour frame of the action by reminding the audience of historical events which they knew were to come later (cf. *Cinna,* 1753 ff.). Camille's words must be meant to refer in part to the Roman Civil Wars, in part perhaps to the eventual fall of the Empire; but Corneille makes them confused and imprecise. She wants to see all this and then die — *of pleasure.* To a Roman like Horace, this is the last word in blasphemy. He kills her.

At this violent climax it is unfortunately necessary to slow things down with a few comments.

When Horace says, 'ma patience à la raison fait place' (1319), we can agree that he has shown patience: can we accept his appeal to reason? Since the abandonment of Lanson's view of the Cornelian *généreux* (see p. 22), this line has given trouble. Here if anywhere, surely, especially if we are ever to forgive Horace, we must believe that he acted in passion. His father will say so ('Un premier mouvement', 1648). A critical remark on a later seventeenth-century poet and critic, Boileau, may help us here: Boileau frequently appeals to reason when it is possible to wonder if he does not mean personal prejudice; but for him, explains Jules Brody,[4] the word does not imply anything like the cold use of logic, but an intuitive 'sense of rightness', which 'had more to do with the expression *avoir raison* than with the verb *raisonner'.* Among the definitions in Littré, backed by quotations from the seventeenth century, are 'Ce qui est de devoir, de droit,

---

[3] We cannot fail to note the four consecutive exclamations where each line begins with 'Rome'; and the optatives, introduced by repeated use of 'que', which fill the rest of the speech, leading up to the final 'Puissé-je ... voir ... voir ... voir . . en être cause, et mourir *de plaisir!*' All this is reinforced by the versification. See *Note on French Prosody,* p. 71.

[4] *Boileau and Longinus* (Genève: Droz, 1958), p. 74.

d'équité, de justice. Ce qui est raisonnable'. Horace says, in effect, 'It can't be right that I should have to put up with this any longer'.

Corneille shirks showing the actual blow. We may regret it; it may be a good thing normally to keep battles, brawls, and even assassinations off the stage (not so much for practical reasons as to preserve a high level of dignity and decorum); but here we have been through a scene which shows the final climactic collision of characters representing the two opposing motives and principles in the play, the climax is reached, and the climax cannot be shown. Corneille lets Horace draw his sword — and later in the much amended edition of 1660 he withdraws even that concession: 'mettant l'épée à la main' becomes 'mettant la main à l'épée' (1319). Camille, who has stood up to him till now, and desires death, is made to run away — on account of 'la frayeur, si naturelle au sexe' *(Examen),* if we can believe that. She who has just reached a frenzy of defiance, calls out 'Ah! traître!' as if she never expected he would hit her; but it is convenient that we should hear some cry to show that he had (and for Corneille a cry has to be in words). He surely regretted having to do this; it simply shows how strong stage decorum, *les bienséances,* had become. The rule was modern, peculiar to France; it banned not only all violent action, but even the drawing of a sword on the stage. (Racine forgot this in the early drafts of his first play, and his friends made him change the passage, *La Thébaïde* IV. 3 — so he says in a letter of November 1663.) The rule is not in antiquity; the *Ars poetica* of the Roman poet Horace is much more lenient (179-88). And it had come in very suddenly; for up to 1635 Corneille had not observed it (*Médée* and *L'Illusion comique* both show deaths on stage).

We have now seen how the murder came about, we can read Horace's own laconic justification (IV. 6), and we shall look more closely at the judgements of the other characters later; none of them will say that he did right. We come back to the question — what exactly happened in Horace's mind and emotions?

He had won a victory at great cost, by refusing to think of the cost. He can hardly go on refusing — Camille is determined he shall not — but what more natural than that, as tension falls, he should dwell on the victory, to fight down other, very bitter thoughts? What more natural than that he should be strained, declamatory, easily thrown off balance? Isn't Camille? And she has no act of her own to regret.

Louis Herland (cf. p. 22; *22,* pp. 146 ff.) has helped understanding of Horace here also by the imaginative way in which he makes this point. True, he goes to extremes and claims to see in him once again what Corneille never expressed, and what, on his own reading, Horace was never consciously aware of — that he is at this moment 'fou de douleur', repressing, stifling the memory of the friend he killed and the rankling fear that he was wrong to do it, that he should have taken the opportunity to decline the fight. He could, given time and tact, have shown Camille that he shared her grief; but Camille finds the raw spot, and jabs it once too often. Corneille does possess an intuitive sense of motives for action which neither his characters nor he himself could explain (he proves it in the sudden decisions of Auguste, *Cinna* V. 3, and Polyeucte, *Pol.* II. 5-6). My only real doubt about this explanation is the extreme, and rather modern, sensibility he requires us to see in the hero.

Corneille has taken a grave source of moral conflict, which always exists potentially in real life — the rival claims of the large human group, the state, against the smallest, the family or the couple of lovers; and found a historical situation in which it reaches its most dramatic intensity. The conflicting and balancing attempts at a solution give a wonderfully complete view of the possibilities. He does not show a fully successful way of surmounting the ordeal; he finds, I think, that there is none. Not Camille's, which is passionate, spontaneous, but egotistical; not Sabine's or her brother's, for their search for a middle way only makes them ineffectual — translated into dramatic terms, makes them insipid if not eventually boring; and not Horace's, though it is intensely dramatic because extreme; but look where it lands him.

So what is the author trying to say? What is his solution,
his 'message', about a very real problem? Surely none; and
surely this makes his play much greater than if it had been a
piece of propaganda for patriotism (or pacifism). He is interested in drama (I shall ask later whether we may not also
say 'in tragedy'), and this requires large-scale, strongly-drawn
human characters locked in conflicts of great tension, which
must strike us, the audience, as real in the sense that they are
true to reality, as in our own lives we experience or observe
it. He seeks for problems, he does not seem ever to have felt
it was his duty as a dramatist to lay down model answers.
'The play is first and foremost a revelation of character in
conflict. It is not an illustration of a set of ideas', as W. G.
Moore has well said (*29, p.* 383). As D. G. Charlton has
conclusively shown (*31*), Corneille assented to the widespread
belief of his time that it was well to teach, as well as please,
in drama; but he denied that it was necessary. The only
necessary thing was to give pleasure — the right kind of pleasure, which is not at all the same as light entertainment.

It was a pleasure that included philosophical insight. For
this study of people in two small states at war is so truly
drawn, despite what may seem to be exaggerations, that we
in the twentieth century can easily read it, if we wish, as an
anti-war play, showing up the ugliness and cruelty of egotism
and material ambition on a national scale — what our modern
world calls imperialism (and still practises). Corneille can have
had no idea that was what he was writing. Alba, for him, was
right in trying to survive and dominate; but so was her enemy,
Rome. It was never wrong to expand if you could; it was fine
if you could help your country to do so; the 'right of conquest'
was a legal right (is still, I suppose, or where is the legitimacy
of our remaining monarchies?), and the only people with any
right to complain — if indeed they had — were those who got
crushed. Sabine, who reveals all this in her speech about the
nascent empire of Rome, would have been the first to cheer
(she says so, 45 ff.) if Rome had not taken her own country

as her first victim. Neither she nor any other character in seventeenth-century fiction, nor any seventeenth-century author I can think of, ever sees the point. But in *Horace,* unknowingly, Corneille makes it. That is why I called the play great.

4

The Action of *Horace*

LIKE *Le Cid* which Corneille had just written, like all tragi-comedies (at least up to then), and like Shakespeare who belongs to that European tradition as much in *Romeo and Juliet* and *Macbeth* as in *As You Like It* or *A Winter's Tale, Horace* has a plot of the kind that has been called 'linear' — it starts at the beginning and goes on till the end. 'La règle des vingt-quatre heures' is kept without too much difficulty, for it is not absurd to place the fight a few hours away from the truce: though Dionysius does say clearly that Horace was tried the day after.

The story is quite elaborate, all the same, and what is more Corneille makes the most of every turning-point for effects of surprise and contrast — relief after anxiety, deeper gloom after relief. Camille, who sees the whole series as a series of blows aimed at her personally, sums it up accurately and vividly:

> En vit-on jamais un [un sort] dont les rudes traverses
> Prissent en moins de rien tant de faces diverses,
> Qui fût doux tant de fois, et tant de fois cruel,
> Et portât tant de coups avant le coup mortel?
> Vit-on jamais une âme en un jour plus atteinte
> De joie et de douleur, d'espérance et de crainte,
> Asservie en esclave à plus d'événements,
> Et le piteux jouet de plus de changements?
> Un oracle m'assure, un songe m'épouvante;
> La bataille m'effraie, et la paix me contente.
> Mon hymen se prépare, et presque en un moment
> Pour combattre mon frère on choisit mon amant;
> Les deux camps mutinés un tel choix désavouent,
> Ils rompent la partie, et les dieux la renouent.
> Rome semble vaincue, et seul des trois Albains

Curiace en mon sang n'a point trempé ses mains.
Dieux! sentais-je point lors des douleurs trop légères,
Pour le malheur de Rome, et la mort de deux frères,
Me flattais-je point trop quand je croyais pouvoir
L'aimer encor sans crime et nourrir quelque espoir?
Sa mort m'en punit bien, et la façon cruelle
Dont mon âme éperdue en reçoit la nouvelle:
Son rival me l'apprend...   (1203)

As she says at the opening, a war was on (whereas in the
historical sources it never started, but was avoided by the
truce; but Corneille wants something more impressive — there
have been two years of 'légers combats', 69, 175, 1492). The
truce stops it; Curiace can visit Camille, their wedding is an-
nounced, and Act I ends in rejoicing. But then champions have
to be chosen, and Corneille is not too much in a hurry to
divide this episode into two, so that Horace knows he is
chosen, then Curiace. There is hope again, when the two
armies stop the fight. The champions refuse to be made to look
like cowards; so the gods are consulted; the gods finally say
'go on'.

The fight itself is decided by the spectacular ruse, related
later by Valère. The historians make much of this, and exploit
the suspense, anxiety, and gratified surprise it can create in
a Roman reader. But Corneille cannot show a fight. Cleverly,
he devises his own *ruse de théâtre* to reproduce the effect of
the other. As Horace turns to run, Julie, the only member of
his household who was there to watch, dashes away also, to
tell the awful news; and she arrives home (a chilling contrast
which Camille omits to mention because it means nothing to
her) at the very moment when her father is explaining that
Rome cannot lose, because the gods have promised her do-
minion over all the earth (III. 6). The value of this dramatic
trick of the incomplete narration is enormous — for now,
though Horace won his fight, we know what his father would
have done if he had not; we owe to it that electric quarter-line,
in which a true Roman says without hesitation what he would
have wished for his only surviving son, outnumbered in com-

bat — 'Qu'il mourût' (1021, words weakened a little, but not ruined, by the line that follows).

The device of the false combat report has been copied again and again since Corneille invented it here (twice by Racine, in the dénouements of *La Thébaïde* and *Mithridate*).

But after this comes the greatest of all the reversals in the play, when Horace dishonours himself by killing his sister. Then, from this point, the play undeniably seems to fall off. The brilliant heroics are over, the forceful emotions spent; and yet the situation is not cleared up, so it cannot be allowed to end. Almost everyone has seen the fifth act as an anticlimax.

But it is arguable that we should see the change as occurring earlier, and talk of a break between Acts III and IV; and two disconcerting features, not one, which disturb the total impression of the play. One in the fourth act, where the triumphant victor almost immediately commits a second violent act, unexpected this time, which leaves him in a very different light; and one in the fifth act, the place where normally the tone rises or is sustained to a full close — whereas here it drops badly, as Horace's life comes to depend on nothing more than a legalistic wrangle.

Corneille felt this. In his *Examen* for the 1660 edition, he puts the case in his own more technical terms:

> Cette mort [de Camille] fait une action double, par le second péril où tombe Horace après être sorti du premier. L'unité de péril d'un héros dans une tragédie fait l'unité d'action; et quand il en est garanti, la pièce est finie... Cette chute d'un péril en l'autre, sans nécessité, fait ici un effet d'autant plus mauvais, que d'un péril public, où il y va de tout l'Etat, il tombe en un péril particulier, où il n'y va que de sa vie, et pour dire encore plus, d'un péril illustre, où il ne peut succomber que glorieusement, en un péril infâme, dont il ne peut sortir sans tache.

He adds that it is also a fault that Camille takes in this second part of the play a prominence she never had in the first, where Sabine seemed the more important of the women.

Corneille's first point of self-accusation is a matter of Unity of Action. If, as he says, the action of a tragedy consists in the hero getting into a peril (of death, or something as bad) and getting out of it again (or not, as the case may be — it had long been held that all tragedies end unhappily), then to have a single action, you must have a single peril: *Horace* has two.

Three of his plays in a line give this impression of being broken-backed. *Le Cid* opens with Rodrigue having to decide to avenge the family honour, though it means fighting the father of his beloved; but when he has done that, the spotlight shifts to the girl, Chimène, who feels it necessary to maintain her honour in the same way by demanding Rodrigue's death. This is a different subject, though it is parallel to the first, a kind of symmetrical opposition. (We need not speak of that other irrelevance, the defeat of a Moorish invasion which makes Rodrigue a national hero overnight, and which Corneille admitted to be a fault: it was the luckiest coincidence for the young man that, for no reason at all, it came just when it did.) In the play after *Horace, Cinna,* the spotlight for three acts is on a set of conspirators plotting to assassinate the emperor Augustus; when they are betrayed and arrested, it turns on the emperor, who has to decide what to do with them. His final magnanimity, after a mental struggle vividly portrayed, forms the dénouement and leaves him the real hero of the play.

I believe the broken back is a result of Corneille's love of taking us all round the subject (as we have seen him do in *Horace*) and exploring all its aspects. In a 'linear' play, this means appearing to change the subject; but Corneille and his contemporaries quickly found that not many 'linear' subjects can be crowded into twenty-four hours, and they learned the alternative method of presenting an explosive situation with roots in the past, which is just about to blow up — there is only time to show the last move or two which lead directly to the detonation; the rest has to be explained as having already happened. In this 'endgame' type of play, where the moves that take place are studied with care, it is possible to shift the spotlight in each act from one character to another — the method may make for complication if there are too many characters whose thoughts and motives call for attention (Corneille's later work was accused of this), but that is a different kind of disadvantage.

Corneille goes on to blame this 'second péril' for coming 'sans nécessité' — for there are cases (like Rodrigue's) where the hero is not safe and sound after facing his first, but finds he must go on to another crisis. This verdict is over-severe, for Camille was determined to meet Horace and challenge him. But Corneille was always scrupulous, for the sake of what was termed *vraisemblance,* to avoid any appearance of coincidence contrived for the convenience of the author: he planted references to what was coming as carefully as a detective-story writer plants his clues; the reader is not meant to see them, but he cannot say afterwards that they were not there. Corneille himself, just before the passage I have quoted, points out that he had emphasised 'la vertu farouche d'Horace' and 'la défense qu'il fait à sa sœur de regretter qui que ce soit, de lui ou de son amant, qui meure au combat'. But he feels this was not enough. Perhaps, as I suggested (p. 39-40), the lack of a scene showing Horace's state of mind after the fight is important here.

Corneille's third point is the most important: Horace falls from 'un péril illustre' into 'un péril infâme'. The change of tone is a disastrous one: the second killing cancels the effect of the first; and it means that the fifth act, which should satisfy and compose our emotions after a stirring action, becomes, of necessity and almost literally, a post-mortem on the ugly action that followed the first. There is a possible defence (for Corneille, not for Horace). Corneille does not use it in the *Examen,* but he puts it — rather too briefly, perhaps — into the mouth of Horace's judge, the king, who says in his summing-up:

> Ce crime quoique grand, énorme, inexcusable,
> Vient de la même épée et part du même bras
> Qui me fait aujourd'hui maître de deux Etats.   (1740)

Is not this a case of something I speak of elsewhere — our author's love of paradox? He has said of another of his plays that it was a surprising and improbable event that made him choose it in the first place (see below, p. 65). The two killings by Horace are both in the historical sources; he says himself in the *Examen* that Camille's death was too well known to omit. I do not think it is too much to conclude that he chose the story, not in spite of, but because of that baffling event. If we can once admit it was not an unfortunate miscalculation of Corneille, we can look on the episode as throwing a valuable new light on the play and the hero. It corrects the short-sighted view that makes Horace a paragon of virtue, an example for us all. It deepens the tragedy, or perhaps creates it (see chap. 5).

I shall therefore end this chapter by looking at the debate which the author thought important enough to fill his last act. What I have said of its loss of dramatic effectiveness is borne out also by the great length of the speeches; but there is at least some drama in the clash of Valère's accusations with the father's defence; while the son refuses to plead, Sabine makes her last intervention (which I will not examine again here), and the king at last gives the awaited summing-up and verdict.

The most important thing that comes out of the debate is surely that no one fails to condemn what Horace did. Even his father, who takes the most favourable view, had admitted in private (1411 ff.) that, though Camille deserved death, Horace should not have killed her and dishonoured himself by doing so; though he makes no such admission before Tulle, and matches Valère's specious hyperboles —

> Quel sang épargnera ce barbare vainqueur ...?
> ....
> Il a sur nous un droit et de mort et de vie (1501, 1508)

— with equally dubious contentions:

> Un premier mouvement ne fut jamais un crime, (1648)

and

> ... Ce bras paternel
> L'aurait déjà puni s'il était criminel   (1657)

(where we remember that he had told his son in private that he spared him 'pour ne se pas punir,' 1438).

Horace himself gives the impression of being emotionally exhausted and deflated, which is likely enough; or else he sees that he will gain nothing by trying to defend the indefensible. As earlier to his father ('Disposez de mon sort', 1419), he says to Tulle that he recognises his absolute authority and is willing to accept the death sentence. His disabused view, now, of the nature of the *gloire* he has won corrects some of our earlier impressions, as it seems to correct his own earlier beliefs.

For he appears to take a decidedly low (and morally unacceptable) view, making glory or honour simply the judgement of 'le peuple' (the *common* people), which is always faulty (1559 ff.) because it judges on results and they do not reflect the degree of *vertu* displayed (1555-1568). They did in his victory — about which he is not bashful — but a similar occasion will never reappear, and so his reputation is bound to fall with time, unless he withdraws from action and from life itself (1572, 1579-82). In fact, he has lost a lot already.

Is this what he really thinks? If so, the value of the motive which he allowed to override so many other claims is severely depreciated; for he does not say here, nor does he seem to think, that there is a value in doing one's duty and serving one's country, regardless of what people may say. That was the defence I thought it right to put forward earlier on his behalf (p. 31): has he proved me wrong? I fancy that, whether or not this is how he really feels in his moment of dejection, he is using the argument because it suits him, rather than because it reflects a deep conviction. Horace is not perhaps the sort of character with whom we associate mental agility; but Corneille may make any of his characters do it (compare Sabine), using, as I said, sound arguments if possible, but worse ones if necessary, and no doubt justifying the insincerity of the words by the intention for which they were used. Chi-

mène, who argues a lot in *Le Cid,* and even swaps arguments
where necessary, is a prime example of this. The attack on
the idea of glory suits Horace here because it gives him a
plausible reason for acquiescing in death, if that is the sentence
that is coming, without at all admitting that it was a just
punishment, and therefore with less ignominy; his last words
are:

> Permettez, ô grand roi, que de ce bras vainqueur
> Je m'immole à ma gloire, et non pas à ma sœur.   (1593)

His father is left to set the issue to rights and defend what
the son had refused to. In the matter of *gloire* he does not
upset more than necessary the premisses of the latter's argument. He does not say, as moralists would say today and
as some were saying even in Corneille's time, that human
glory is worthless and may be morally evil, but virtue is a
different thing. He simply says that there are enlightened judges
whose opinion is of real value. (With the social values of the
seventeenth century, these must be the privileged classes who
alone can attain to *générosité.*)

> C'est aux rois, c'est aux grands, c'est aux esprits bien faits
> A voir la vertu pleine en ses moindres effets,
> C'est d'eux seuls qu'on reçoit la véritable gloire,
> Eux seuls des vrais héros assurent la mémoire.   (1717)

Tulle's summing-up will not wholly please those who take
sides for Horace, or those who condemn him. He asserts his
'vertu' and his 'crime', both of which he calls exceptional; and
if he comes down on the side of pardon (1760) — for it is
pardon and not acquittal, since in law no amount of 'vertu'
can wipe out one crime — it is partly because Horace has
done so much for him (and Rome), just as in *Le Cid* Rodrigue
had been cleared of homicide because he had saved Spain (the
claims of the state, already); it is also because justice in Rome
has turned a blind eye before, in the case of her founder
himself (1756). Cynicism? Rather, perhaps, a deeply tragic
realism of judgement. Even here (and we may say even in

Médée, his first tragedy), Corneille shows himself anxious to see and reveal the realities that are the foundation of power-politics.

We may incline to be more severe than Rome was towards Horace; and it is possible to look with more compassion on Camille than her family did, because we may look on her 'crime' less harshly. Tulle pitied her (1777); Corneille allowed both versions of his tragedy (the longer original, of 1794 lines, and that of 1656, which lacks the last twelve lines) to end with a pathetic allusion to her 'reunion' with Curiace. In any case, we know more about her and her motives than her family did, because we have heard her monologue. But Corneille could have found ways of increasing or decreasing her degree of guilt if he had wanted to. He was not primarily concerned to make the punishment fit the crime, but to make his personages struggle and suffer. That is what serious drama lives on. The tortures Corneille makes her enumerate so movingly were the tortures he had devised for her. Only in melodrama do the just and the unjust all get their exact deserts.

It is not in this sense that Corneille tried to balance his effects. But in the sense in which I have used the idea of symmetry, this act completes the impression created by the whole play, of equal (or nearly equal) and opposing motives between which it has been hard for the characters, and now is just as hard for their king and for the spectators of the play, to strike a just balance.

5

Tragedy

CORNEILLE spoke of all his plays as 'poèmes dramatiques' — i. e., verse compositions written to be acted. They also deserve the word 'dramatique' in the narrower sense used by critics — they show people in changing situations that give rise to conflict between them, and suspense in spectators' minds about the outcome.

He called *Horace* and eighteen of his other plays tragedies, implying something in common with the works of the Greeks for which the name was used first. To other plays of his he refused the name; and for one of these, *Don Sanche d'Aragon,* he explained his reason.

> *Don Sanche* est une véritable comédie, quoique tous les acteurs soient ou rois ou grands d'Espagne, puisqu'on n'y voit naître aucun péril par qui nous puissions être portés à la pitié ou à la crainte. Notre aventurier Carlos n'y court aucun risque . . .
>
> *(Dédicace)*

— Except that the risks death in a duel, and suffers the pains of love; but of such things Comedy is full. Some serious peril then, peril of death or, as he says elsewhere (*8*, p. 9) 'de pertes d'Etats, ou de bannissement' (a fate worse than death for a king with a sentiment of *gloire*); to ensure that the action, the issue, was of the utmost gravity. This obviously is hardly enough to go on for a definition. More important, it gives no key to the nature of Greek tragedy, where peril is rarely important and is sometimes absent. We can ask, and no doubt should ask, what it is that makes a tragedy, so that a work without it is not a tragedy, and so that we may call

something tragic which is not in a play but in a novel, a
history, or a newspaper — what French expresses more precisely than English as, not 'une tragédie' nor even 'la tragédie', but 'le tragique'. But we cannot ask this without getting
into very deep waters, and finding that, though any reader
of drama may give his own answer, it is impossible to arrive
at one over which everyone will agree.

The question was never clearly asked in antiquity, or even
in the seventeenth century: people knew *a* tragedy when they
saw it, they might try to describe a class of dramatic works
which could be called 'the tragedy', but they went no further.
Literary genres were Forms before they became Kinds: they
all began by being compositions of a recognisable shape and
length, devised to suit occasions that often occurred — a song
to be sung to a tune, probably for a dance (lyric), a story after
supper in a chief's hall (epic). Even though the occasions
changed with social conditions ('the lyric' has changed vastly,
several times), some Forms found an appropriate subject-
matter or mood — no doubt because certain experiments
proved successful and were imitated — until it became possible
to recognise a theme or mood, even if it occurred in a different
Form, as being lyrical, epic — or of course tragic.

There was not, after all, much to help Corneille and his
age to gain an idea of what they were aiming at; for the social
occasion that had originally given rise to tragedy had long
since disappeared, whatever it had been. A religious ritual
clearly, but about its nature and purpose much has been
conjectured and very little is known.

There were ancient models which Renaissance scholarship
had unearthed: very few really — from Greece, seven tragedies
survive by Æschylus, seven by Sophocles, eighteen by Euripi-
des; from Rome, ten pieces ascribed (one or more, incorrectly)
to Seneca the philosopher. Seneca was much the most influential of these (and the worst), because his Latin was far easier
to read, and seemed more attractive. Corneille knew him well:
Greek plays he had to read in Latin translation.

The one important contribution to the theory of tragedy
from antiquity was the *Poetics* of Aristotle — unknown in the

ancient world (except presumably to the philosopher's inner circle of pupils), rediscovered and published for the first time in 1498, a difficult work which took a long time to understand at all fully. This too is more concerned with the origin and functioning of tragedies than with the essence or spirit of tragedy. One can quote, certainly, short formulas which have been really influential. Tragedy, said Aristotle, arouses 'pity and fear'; through them it brings about 'its purgation of such emotions'. This last phrase (which seems to have denoted a beneficial lowering of emotional tension) was woefully misunderstood by most people up to Corneille's time, and taken to mean that the passions, all of them, were to be purified by tragedy — i.e. it should make men morally better by lessons and examples. A third pregnant suggestion I have already quoted — that the truly tragic situation comes about between friends or kinsmen.

The Middle Ages, which knew much literature in Latin but none in Greek, knew the name tragedy, and the fact that tragedy dealt with the fall of princes (cf. Chaucer's *Monk's Tale* and its prologue). The other notions on the subject which it passed on to the Renaissance have been usefully summarised by Lanson (*23,* p. 5) in four points: tragedy differs from comedy in being 'royale' (tragic characters were the great ones of the earth, whose fall involved their kingdoms; comic characters were not), 'historique' (you found the stories in history or legend, as you would expect; ordinary people's lives are not in history, the stories have to be invented), 'sanglante' (tragedies end in a death or deaths, comedies in a wedding), and 'élevée de style', as was only fitting.

We saw in chapter 1 how the French sixteenth century made what it could out of all this, and the seventeenth greatly enlarged, but also adulterated, the conception. This conception was perfected and crystallised in the theatres of Paris (largely thanks to the example of Corneille) and became what is conventionally called 'la tragédie classique', undergoing little change, as a Form, until it perished in the early nineteenth century under the assault of Romanticism. Since then — ironically, since the time when 'tragedies' ceased to be written at all — esthetic theory has been busy over the question of defining the Kind, and produced dozens of rival definitions, each refusing the title of tragedy to any work that fails to satisfy it, each claiming to embrace the whole field of Attic, Elizabethan and French tragedy, and each, it has to be said, failing to do so because it is too narrow. But the first thing to be said about all such formulas is that, if we seek to apply them to Corneille, we must realise that we are committing an anachronism, since Corneille could not have known them or thought in such terms; and therefore in a sense it is unjust to condemn him if he does not satisfy them. (That in itself does not make them mistaken. A student can choose any one that appeals to him, at his own risk. And it is entirely conceivable that certain aims or inklings of a genius of the past may be better translated now in our more developed modern vocabulary, than he was able to express them even to himself.) What Corneille must himself have thought he was trying to do, is a question I shall return to shortly.

I shall look at two of these modern conceptions; the first, because it takes up a point I made in the first chapter, that French tragedy depends for its shape and its spirit on the mechanism of the plot. This is contrary to the very nature of tragedy, according to a well-known passage in the *Antigone* of Jean Anouilh, which no less a critic than Eugène Vinaver has quoted with approval and used as the basis of part of his own theory: [1]

> C'est propre, la tragédie. C'est reposant, c'est sûr ...
> Dans le drame, avec ses traîtres, avec ses méchants
> acharnés, cette innocence persécutée, ces vengeurs, ces
> terre-neuve, ces lueurs d'espoir, cela devient épouvanta-
> ble de mourir, comme un accident. On aurait peut-être
> pu se sauver, le bon jeune homme aurait peut-être pu
> arriver à temps avec les gendarmes. Dans la tragédie on
> est tranquille. D'abord, on est entre soi. On est tous in-
> nocents en somme! ... Et puis, surtout, c'est reposant, la

---

[1] *Racine et la poésie tragique* (Paris: Nizet, 2e édition, 1963), p. 52.

tragédie, parce qu'on sait qu'il n'y a plus d'espoir, le sale espoir; qu'on est pris, qu'on est enfin pris comme un rat, avec tout le ciel sur son dos.

There is much truth in this, concerning some types of tragedy. Not that anybody suggests that you could write a play of any sort without plot — only that there is tension or opposition between the element of plot and this kind of contemplative emotion. Let us remember however that in Corneille the question that holds us in suspense is never 'Will he, or she, escape?': it is usually something like 'What will he decide to do?' or 'How will he face that?' or 'Will he be tempted to betray his principles *now*?' And a plot is needed to bring up these questions.

On the other hand, the common ground of many modern theorists is that tragedy portrays the limitations of the human condition, where aspirations and desires are thwarted and crushed by some much greater power, called, according to the metaphysical beliefs of the writer and his public, God, Fate, or recently, the impersonal Absurd Universe. Lanson, attempting to describe Attic tragedy (which he did not know very well), puts it thus: 'Le *tragique,* chez les Grecs, était le spectacle et l'émotion *(crainte* ou *pitié)* de la misère humaine; mais de la misère créée par les conditions essentielles de la vie, par la mystérieuse violence de la destinée, par le jeu souvent ironique d'une force, incompréhensible, divine, qui confond l'homme et l'écrase.' *(23,* p. 3).

Geoffrey Brereton, in his sensible and helpful study of the *Principles of Tragedy (27,* pp. 117-18), is less willing to be positive and comes down to this as the only element he finds present in all the great periods and examples: 'curiosity, undogmatic and perhaps irrational but never frivolous, about the nature and sources of power as it affects the human subject.' This power may be of one (or more) of three kinds: 'the power attributed to ... divine forces', or even natural forces so long as they remain in some way mysterious; next, 'forces within the individual', the dangerous and unpredictable passions that motivate him; finally, 'political power', which may be 'dramatised as a story of kings, usurpations and conspiracies', but also 'conceived as the collective power of the community', when it may shade back into the first type.

It is not at all hard to bring *Horace* into a definition as accommodating as this. 'The power of the community', the quasi-religious force of patriotism, clearly triggers off all the actions and passions in the play; admirable or pitiable or terrible forces are unleashed by this within the individuals affected; and even the divine is present, as represented by moral imperatives ('duty').

And also, one might suggest, by the quite frequent appeals of characters to the Roman gods. I have consistently neglected these in my study, because I think it possible, and probably wisest, to look on them as a kind of 'local colour', the only kind Corneille would wish to introduce, because it is wholly within the thoughts of the personages. But Horace himself, with one insignificant exception ('Quelle injustice aux dieux . . .' 1391), speaks only of a very impersonal 'sort':

> . . . Du sort envieux quel que soient les projets . . . (381)
> Le sort qui de l'honneur nous ouvre la barrière . . . (431)
> Querellez ciel et terre, et maudissez le sort . . . (529)

Sabine, who hopes the most constantly to find pity in the gods, is each time disappointed. Her last words on the subject are:

> . . . Je m'imaginais dans la divinité
> Beaucoup moins d'injustice, et bien plus de bonté.
> (933, cf. 760, 828, 839, 857)

There seems to be no clear purpose on Corneille's part to ascribe the way events do turn out to any design of divine providence. The clear ethical implication of the play, it seems to me, as of all his drama, is that the good may well find themselves strengthened in carrying out the right resolves, but that it is entirely up to them to form these resolves and start moving. Much later (*Œdipe,* 1659), he puts this statement into a character's mouth:

Le ciel, juste à punir, juste à récompenser,
Pour rendre aux actions leur peine ou leur salaire,
Doit nous offrir son aide, et puis nous laisser faire. (1168)

Le vieil Horace, who has a stoical belief in an impersonal divine justice —

La prudence des dieux autrement en dispose,
Sur leur ordre éternel mon esprit se repose (979, cf. 1404)

— but certainly believes that the gods protect and favour Rome:

Les dieux à notre Enée ont promis cette gloire   (991)

— says the same thing as the character from *Œdipe* in the energetic last words of Act II:

Faites votre devoir, et laissez faire aux dieux.

There is today a strong tendency to look on Corneille's work as a whole as being a drama of buoyant optimism based on the author's faith in a divine Providence which will infallibly see to it that justice triumphs and wrong is punished (see especially André Stegmann's work, *21*). And this would be to take out of its religious sentiment all the mystery and all the sense of the weakness and vulnerability of man, on which the Brereton theory would make tragedy depend. Much of Corneille's work, and in particular the other masterpieces of his first period *(Le Cid, Cinna, Polyeucte)* seem to bear this out. So do the first three acts of *Horace* (up to IV. 2, to be exact), for the dead, up to that point, are morally victorious since they have died without cowardice or dishonour; but not the fourth, where Camille dies pitiably, but condemned by the prevailing orthodoxy of patriotism, nor certainly the fifth, where Horace is the first to feel that he has tarnished his dearly-won glory.

On that showing *Horace* might be the only 'true tragedy' Corneille ever wrote. But if we are less exacting, and content to abide by the conception of tragedy by which Corneille worked, it is easy to show how both parts of this work fit in. The 'four points' — *royale, historique, sanglante, élevée de style* — with Corneille's own amendment (though he formulated it later) replacing fall and death by grave peril: an action in which personages above the common have to react to a situation above the common, in that it constitutes a threat, a challenge or a test of the most serious kind. Corneille's characters may be morally good or (in certain of his plays) evil, they are usually *généreux* and strong; but some of his contemporaries showed characters passionate and weak, and the formula allows both. The test may be failed, or passed with flying colours (cf. above, pp. 9, 31).

For Horace — the heroic Horace of the first three acts — it is an ordeal which he does not for a moment see as an affliction to be met with dignity and resignation, but as one to be surmounted if he possibly can. Heroism — which has its links with *gloire,* but is not the same thing, since one describes the act for which the other is the recompense — was another idea much in the air in the early seventeenth century, and Corneille was evidently much drawn to it. Four years after our play we find him interchanging the terms *tragique* and *héroïque,* without apparently seeing any difference. (He speaks of trying tragedy after his early comedies, and now, with *Le Menteur,* returning to comedy.) 'Je n'osai me fier à mes seules forces . . . , pour m'élever à la dignité du tragique, je pris l'appui du grand Sénèque . . . quand je me suis résolu de repasser du héroïque au naïf, je . . . me suis laissé conduire au fameux Lope de Vega' (*Epître dédicatoire*).

Later, in 1651, he conceived a heroic type simpler but even stronger than Horace, though it is true Nicomède has no moral dilemma to solve; or rather, he never doubts what he has to do and therefore it is not a dilemma for him. (I refer to the fact that he has every inducement to rebel against his father the king, but never contemplates it.) The increasing certainty of being disinherited, made prisoner by his enemy, perhaps killed, he faces with utter contempt and biting sarcasm, for want of any more material weapon. In the end he comes out victorious, not through his own efforts but mainly through the act of one who has been influenced by his attitude; and then he shows exemplary magnanimity.

> Ce héros de ma façon sort un peu des règles de la tragédie, en ce qu'il ne cherche point à faire pitié par l'excès de ses malheurs: mais le succès a montré que la fermeté des grands cœurs, qui n'excite que de l'admiration dans l'âme du spectateur, est quelquefois aussi agréable que la compassion que notre art nous commande de mendier pour leurs misères *(Au Lecteur)*.

It may well be thought that *Nicomède* is less revolutionary than Corneille claims here. He seems only to be perfecting consciously an appeal he had used a good deal before. Nicomède's *vertu* does differ in degree, and even in kind, from that of Horace (who is more heavily tested); but the keyword Corneille has found to describe his own effect, *admiration* (to replace, as he said on a later occasion, the 'pity and fear' of Aristotle), only echoes what Curiace said in our play:

> ...Cette âpre vertu ne m'était pas connue...
> Souffrez que je l'admire et ne l'imite point.   (504, 06)

Admirer, admiration, carried in the seventeenth century the notion of surprise; Furetière's dictionary (1690) defines it: 'Action par laquelle on regarde avec étonnement quelque chose de grand et de surprenant.' Several times in his theoretical works Corneille uses even stronger terms, such as *éclat* and *éblouissement:* the audience is to be impressed, sometimes even tricked if necessary, by dazzling effects. 'A man of the theatre, Corneille was very conscious of this aspect of his art' (Peter France, *15,* p. 23).

He sought for such effects carefully. Another critic has said that when reading history to find suggestions for plots, he looked for 'paradoxes' (in the etymological sense of what went clean against everyone's expectations), the unlooked-for act, 'les records de ce que peut atteindre dans les différentes directions la nature humaine' (Valdemar Vedel, *12,* p. 191.) He admitted, in the *Examen* of another play (*Pertharite,* 1651-52) that 'Ce qui l'a fait avorter au théâtre a été *l'événement extraordinaire qui me l'avait fait choisir',* which was that of a dethroned king forgetting his *gloire* and seeking to trade his useless claim against his wife's liberation. (An additional joke here is that Corneille must have forgotten this interesting detail was not in the sources at all, but an invention of his own.)

He had been driven into making a principle out of this search for 'l'événement extraordinaire', and finding theoretical justifications for it, by the arguments which had been used against *Le Cid:* there, the heroine continues to love the man who has killed her father, and Corneille was told it was not only immoral, but contrary to *vraisemblance,* for a well-brought-up young lady to do any such thing. The story was true (true to tradition, anyway);

> Mais nous maintenons que toutes les vérités ne sont pas bonnes pour le théâtre . . . . C'est principalement en ces rencontres que le poète a droit de préférer la vraisemblance à la vérité, et de travailler plutôt sur un sujet feint et raisonnable que sur un [sujet] véritable qui ne fût pas conforme à la raison. (*Sentiments de l'Académie,* in *8,* p. 203)

Only in 1647 did Corneille print his defence, when publishing a later tragedy, *Héraclius,* which had also been accused of *invraisemblance.* He replies that here too the detail in question was true to history (or true enough!), and that the remark about *vraisemblance* in Aristotle's *Poetics* does not apply to the subject of a play, but only its *disposition* (the way the events are made to hang together). 'J'irai plus outre; et quoique peut-être on voudra prendre cette proposition pour un paradoxe, je ne craindrai point d'avancer que le sujet d'une belle tragédie doit n'être pas vraisemblable' (*Au Lecteur, 8,* p. 190, or *6,* p. 440). In 1660 he leads off his *Discours du poème dramatique* with a similar statement — technical *vraisemblance* is only one of the ways of making an audience accept a story (which is what matters), and what is *vraisem-blable* is often just too dull.

> Ce n'est pas qu'on ne puisse faire une tragédie d'un sujet purement vraisemblable ... ; mais les grands sujets qui remuent fortement les passions, et en opposent l'impétuosité aux lois du devoir ou aux tendresses du sang [kinship], doivent toujours aller au-delà du vraisemblable, et ne trouveraient aucune croyance parmi les auditeurs, s'ils n'étaient soutenus, ou par l'autorité de l'histoire qui persuade avec empire [power, conviction], ou par la préoccupation de l'opinion commune qui nous donne ces mêmes auditeurs déjà tous persuadés [i.e., the preconceived notions in the average man's mind, thanks to which our audience already accepts the story]. Il n'est pas vraisemblable que Médée tue ses enfants, que Clytemnestre assassine son mari, qu'Oreste poignarde sa mère; mais l'histoire le dit, et la représentation de ces grands crimes ne trouve point d'incrédules. Il n'est ni vrai ni vraisemblable qu'Andromède, exposée à un monstre marin, ait été garantie de ce péril par un cavalier volant, qui avait des ailes aux pieds; mais c'est une fiction que l'antiquité a reçue, et comme elle l'a transmise jusqu'à nous, personne ne s'en offense quand il la voit sur le théâtre. (*8*, p. 2)

In other words, Corneille needed 'l'extraordinaire' for his kind of tragedy; but the members of his audience must be willing not to question it, either because they believed it had happened in history, or because it was a part of the Greek legends they had learnt at school.

He could see that he had found such a 'grand sujet' before he started work on the story of the Horatii. 'L'auteur dont je l'ai tirée,' he tells Richelieu in the dedication, '... commence à décrire cette fameuse histoire par ce glorieux éloge, "qu'il n'y a presque aucune chose plus noble dans toute l'antiquité" '. That sentence comes from Livy (I. xxiv; *9*, p. 83); the other source, Dionysius, ends his account with a sentence which Corneille could not have missed: the incidents, he says, 'showed some remarkable and unexpected reversals of fortune'

(III. xxii; *10*, p. 93). The word here translated 'remarkable' is, literally, 'wonderful, marvellous' and reminds us again of 'admiration'; the word translated 'unexpected' is literally 'paradoxical'; the word for 'reversals' is the word *peripeteia*, made familiar to all French students of the *Poetics* as 'péripétie'. Our playwright must have seen two brilliant paradoxes crying out to be used — the brothers-in-law who agree to fight each other to the death and refuse to be let off, and even more, the national hero who 'de la même épée' and with the same motive, comes straight home after winning his fight, to kill his sister.

As for the 'tragic' Horace of the last two acts, there is little doubt about his case. He can easily be seen as a classic instance of pride going before a fall, *hubris* followed by *nemesis*. Dionysius indeed says so. 'It was ordained that even he, as he was but mortal, should not be fortunate in everything, but should feel some stroke of the envious power who, having from an insignificant man made him great in a brief moment and raised him to wonderful and unexpected distinction [the same two Greek epithets again], plunged him into the unhappy state of being his sister's murderer' (III. xx; *10*, p. 79).

Is this why Corneille, seeing a paradox to be exploited, has puzzled us all ever since by giving his heroic figure a sombre tragic side such as we shall not find again in his work for a long time? Surely he must have flung himself upon it with joy; but was there not another reason too? The supposed rule of the unhappy ending for tragedy still held the field, and had not yet been challenged in the modern world. Corneille had observed it in his first tragedy, *Médée,* where the heroine does not herself die but kills her two children to be revenged on their father. When he did challenge it, the public acclaim for the first, heroic Horace may have been what emboldened him. In *Cinna,* a year more or less after, there is, as I have said, a pardon and a reconciliation with not a drop of blood shed. Meanwhile, seen from our distance, *Horace* looks curiously ambiguous and 'broken-backed'.

To prove that it was the heroic note which struck the imagination of all, we have only to read his contemporaries.

Madame de Sévigné was twenty years younger than Corneille, and probably would not have seen *Horace* in its first season, but she remained devoted to him after he had changed his style and lost the favour of the public. In 1672, when his rival Racine was in his heyday, she writes to her daughter about Racine's play, *Bajazet,* the most exciting, in the sense of danger and violence, that he ever wrote. She had seen it, and half liked it, but found fault with the characters and the plot.

> Il y a pourtant des choses agréables; et rien de parfaitement beau, rien qui enlève, point de ces tirades de Corneille qui font frissonner . . . Vive donc notre vieil ami Corneille! Pardonnons-lui de méchants vers, en faveur des divines et sublimes beautés qui nous transportent; ce sont des traits de maître qui sont inimitables (16 mars 1672).

'Ces tirades . . . qui font frissonner, . . . qui nous transportent'! When I analysed them in the preceding chapters, this thrill was probably muffled by my commentary. It is a pity, and yet of course it is necessary to grasp fully what is being said before one can thrill to the emotional impact. (The seventeenth century did not have this trouble: the style and language were of its own day.) But of course the impact is the thing; and I might have given more attention to the rhetorical art of Corneille's verse, the building of climaxes, the antitheses that strike sparks like duellists' rapiers, were it not that that could have muffled the impact just as effectively.

More even than the great tirades, some of his contemporaries seem to have treasured those lines or fragments of lines in which, without visible rhetoric, without figures of speech or at least without obvious figures of speech, a heroic — and surprising — thought, prompted by the challenge of a crisis, is matched by its exact and perfect expression, and carries an electric charge. There is of course enormous art in finding this exact equivalent in a small space, and then concealing the effort of doing so. There are not many such passages in the whole of Corneille; there are two in *Horace* — 'Je ne vous connais plus. — Je vous connais encore . . .'; and even more the spontaneous cry of the old father saying his son would have been better dead than escaped: 'Qu'il mourût!'.

Boileau quoted this as the best example he knew in French of that 'sublimity' in thought which had been praised as the greatest beauty in literature by the late-Greek critic (wrongly identified with Longinus) whom he had just translated.

> Le Sublime . . . ne persuade pas proprement, mais il ravit, il transporte, et produit en nous une certaine admiration mêlée d'étonnement et de surprise, qui est toute autre chose que de plaire seulement, ou de persuader . . . Mais quand le Sublime vient à éclater où il faut, il renverse tout comme un foudre, et présente d'abord [= at once] toutes les forces de l'orateur ramassées ensemble. (*Traité du Sublime*, chap. 1. See also the end of Boileau's preface.)

This planner of emotive shocks may seem a far cry from the stiff and rather solemn Corneille of my first chapter. Whoever can respond to them both can believe that he understands the greatness of this dramatist and (in a real sense) poet. The first is the essential one, the poet whom the second laboured to produce. So much excitement and emotion may not seem to fit the idea handed down by our elders of what 'the classical ideal' was all about (but happily that idea has now been much eroded). If they do not, so much the better. Corneille did not know he had to exemplify a classical ideal. He was creating it; and if it got rather dull after his time, what wonder? It lasted two hundred years.

APPENDIX I

Tragedy in France before *Horace*

First phase (second half of sixteenth century): amateur compositions for invited audiences, based on Seneca, the only ancient model easily available. The plot is often simply a catastrophe expected, then arriving; the speeches are laments, pleas, moralisings, the characters almost uniformly passive. What we call drama is still to be rediscovered; some aspects are still to be invented.

Second phase (the 1620s): the theatre, professional now, becomes popular with Paris society as the disturbances of the religious wars give way to civilised pursuits. A taste for a plot providing suspense — a hero in danger but eventually escaping — is catered for by a new genre called tragicomedy. The suspense and the happy ending had been absent from sixteenth-century tragedy — they come from comedy. The love-interest, also prominent in tragicomedy, comes from medieval romance by way of the prose novel, then very popular.

Third phase (the 1630s): from Italy comes renewed interest in the Unities of Time and Place, which had been observed in phase 1 and forgotten before phase 2 started. They must have made the adventure-plots of tragicomedy very hard to contrive, but tragedy seemed more amenable. In the winter 1634-35 two new tragedies respecting the 24-hour limit give tragedy a new lease of life. Corneille had written comedies from 1629, and one unsuccessful tragicomedy in 1631-32. His tragedy *Médée* (1635), after Seneca, follows the new trend; then he returns to tragicomedy with *Le Cid,* which is the only French masterpiece in the genre. But now he turns back to tragedy with *Horace* (1640).

Note on French Prosody

The alexandrine metre which Corneille uses produced, in less skilled hands, a rather dreary run of twelve syllables, the last marked by a rhyme and some kind of stress, usually the end of a sentence or clause. A slightly weaker break cut the line in the middle; the sense had to provide justifications for the stresses and breaks as best it could. The reason why stress cannot be spoken of without reference to 'breaks' or 'pauses' is a peculiarity of French intonation — in French, words do not carry their own invariable stresses as in other languages, nor can a word be picked out for emphasis, irrespective of its position (as English can do by italicising). What carries stress is the last fully-sounded syllable of a breath-group, the breath-group being a group of syllables pronounced in one outlet of breath, and separated from the next, not necessarily by a silence, but by a recognisable grouping, or 'phrasing', as a musician would call it. Camille wishes Horace to become so unhappy that he even envies *her* (1292), but she cannot say:

Que tu tombes au point de *me* porter envie.

Even if the breath-group 'de me porter envie' could be broken, 'me' contains an 'e muet', which may never bear stress. Camille could only say 'de me porter envie/ A moi//' — giving rise to a sensational *enjambement* such as Corneille would not have dared, or perhaps wished, to use. He has preferred to keep the stress in the normal place, on 'envie', which gives a very similar sense ('not to pity, but actually to envy, me').

Corneille's secret, in his most vigorous verse, seems to be to conceive his thoughts in the patterns of balance or contrast that we have already noted (p. 16), and to translate those patterns of thought into patterns of rhythm, making sound and sense reinforce each other. He can never neglect the stress at the twelfth syllable, without which the line would not be recognisable as such; there is always some stress on the sixth; but there may be one or even more other stresses which are stronger in the first half of the line (less often in the second). (Just which stresses should be made the strongest is often a matter of personal feeling.) Later in the century, Racine will find much more subtle and flexible effects: Corneille finds simple and rather geometrical rhythms adequate for his bold but logical thought.

In Camille's last speech, 'Rome' is as prominent metrically as it is rhetorically:

> Ro//me, l'unique objet/ de mon ressentiment!//
> Ro//me à qui vient ton bras/ d'immoler/ mon amant!//
> Ro//me qui t'a vu naî//tre et que ton cœur/ ado//re!
> Ro//me enfin que je hais// parce qu'elle t'hono//re!
>
>   (1301)

In the first two lines, perhaps also the third, no other word receives a comparable stress. The fourth line, with three violent stresses, including the symmetrical antithesis 'hais . . . honore', restores balance.

There are few other departures in *Horace* from the fairly symmetrical line hinged in the centre; but their rarity gives them value. Two occur in *le vieil Horace*'s moment of anguish (III. 6):

> Que vouliez-vous qu'il fît/ contre trois?//
>   — Qu'il mourût//   (1021)

(No division in the first half: two strong stresses — rarely found — in the second.)

> Pleurez/ l'au//tre, pleurez/ l'irrépara/ble affront//   (1017)

Here, both words 'pleurez' are emphatic, but the meaning seems to give 'l'autre' even more stress.)

Corneille in his Literary and Historical Setting

A Chronological Sketch

1552 First original tragedy written in French: Etienne Jodelle, *Cléopâtre captive.*

1562-98 Religious wars in France.

1568-83 Publication of 7 tragedies by Robert Garnier, the greatest representative of the first (Renaissance) phase; 3 subjects come from Roman history, 3 from themes of ancient tragedies, 1 from the Old Testament.

1589 Accession of Henri IV.

1606 Corneille born in Rouen.

1610 Accession of Louis XIII.

1623-28 Publication of 34 plays by Alexandre Hardy, a playwright under contract to the company using the Hôtel de Bourgogne theatre since about 1595. He claimed to have written 500 or 600 plays. Of the 34, 12 are tragedies and 14 tragicomedies; unlike earlier tragedies, these plays generally ignore the unities of time and place.

1629 Corneille's first play, *Mélite,* a comedy, produced in Paris by the rivals of the Hôtel de Bourgogne, who later settled in the Théâtre du Marais, and produced all his plays till 1647.

1630 *Silvanire,* a pastoral by Jean Mairet, renews interest in Paris for the stage unities.

1631 *Clitandre,* an extravagant and unsuccessful tragicomedy; followed, 1631-34, by 4 successful comedies.

1634-35 *Hercule mourant,* tragedy after Seneca by Jean Rotrou, and *Sophonisbe,* tragedy from Roman history after an Italian original, by Mairet, inaugurate a new series of tragedies in Paris.

1635 *Médée,* after Seneca, Corneille's first tragedy.

1635 War between France and Spain. A Spanish army invades France from Flanders.

1636-42 A succession of conspiracies against Cardinal de Richelieu, Louis XIII's minister.

1636 Battle of Corbie; Spanish defeat.

1636 *L'Illusion* (or *L'Illusion comique*), comedy with play-within-play actions.

1636 Corneille obtains the patronage of Richelieu, who is organising literary propaganda for his policies.

1637 *Le Cid,* tragicomedy, the greatest theatrical success so far known in Paris. (In editions from 1648 onwards, the play is called a tragedy.)

1637 'La Querelle du Cid', a war of pamphlets, ended by *Les Sentiments de l'Académie française sur le 'Cid'* (1638), commissioned by Richelieu, with a judgement which Corneille considered unjust.

1640 *Horace,* tragedy (dedicated to Richelieu), produced February-March, at the private theatre in Richelieu's palace, and in May at the Théâtre du Marais (for which see above, under 1629).

1640-42 (dates uncertain) *Cinna* and *Polyeucte,* tragedies.

1641 Corneille marries. He will have 7 children.

1642 Richelieu dies, and his extensive patronage of literature ends with him. He is succeeded by Cardinal Mazarin. 1643 Louis XIII dies. His widow, Anne of Austria, reigns as regent till Louis XIV comes of age.

1643-53 9 more plays, of which 7 are tragedies.

1648-53 La Fronde, a confused period of conspiracies and civil war.

1651-56 *L'Imitation de Jésus-Christ,* verse translation of the well-known devotional work ascribed to Thomas à Kempis. The poem, of over 13000 lines, was a great success.

1658 Molière settles in Paris with his company, until his death in 1673.

1659 *Œdipe,* tragedy: Corneille returns to writing for the theatre under the patronage of Nicolas Foucquet, Surintendant des Finances.

1660 The first collective edition of the plays to contain the three *Discours (Du poème dramatique, De La Tragédie, Des Trois Unités)* and an *Examen* of each play included.

1661 Corneille goes on to produce 10 more plays, 6 of which are tragedies, the last being *Suréna,* 1674.

1661 From the death of Mazarin, Louis XIV rules without a minister, and begins a new policy of state patronage of the arts.

1664-77 Career of Jean Racine as playwright — 9 tragedies and one comedy;

1670 Simultaneous production of his *Bérénice* and Corneille's *Tite et Bérénice,* on the same subject.

1684 Corneille dies in Paris.

Selective Bibliography

EDITIONS

There are numerous editions of *Horace,* and of Corneille's complete, or selected, works. The following can be recommended.

1. Corneille, *Horace,* edited by W. G. Moore (Oxford: Blackwell, 1938). Very short, but excellent introduction; no notes. Text of the first edition, 1641.
2. Corneille, *Horace,* edited by Bernard Masson, Classiques Larousse, (Paris, 1960). In French. Text of the definitive edition, 1682.
3. Corneille, *Horace,* edited with an introduction and notes by Peter H. Nurse, Harrap's French Classics (London, 1963). Text of 1641.
4. Corneille, *Horace,* by P. J. Yarrow, Macmillan's Modern Language Texts (London, 1967). Text of 1682.
5. *Œuvres de P. Corneille,* edited by Ch. Marty-Laveaux, Les Grands Ecrivains de la France; 12 vols. and album (Paris: Hachette, 1862-68). *Horace,* III, 247-358.
6. Corneille, *Œuvres complètes,* préface de Raymond Lebègue, présentation et notes de André Stegmann, l'Intégrale (Paris: Seuil, 1963.)
   The most useful 'complete works'. Text of 1682, without variants.
7. Corneille, *Théâtre complet,* tome I, edited by G. Couton (Paris: Garnier, 1971.)
   This edition, full and reliable for all historical and biographical information, has not so far (1980) progressed beyond the first volume. The other volumes in uniform covers are reprints of the much older edition of Maurice Rat.
8. Pierre Corneille, *Writings on the Theatre,* edited by H. T. Barnwell, Blackwell's French Texts (Oxford, 1965).
   Critical text of the *Discours* and *Examens,* with most of the prefaces, etc., and an excellent introduction on Corneille's aims and theories.

HISTORICAL SOURCES

9. Livy, in fourteen volumes with an English translation by B. O. Foster, The Loeb Classical Library (Cambridge, Mass.: Harvard

U.P. and London: Heinemann, 1919). Vol. I, bk. I, xxiii-xxvi, pp. 77-95.

10. The *Roman Antiquities* of Dionysius of Halicarnassus, with an English translation by Earnest Cary, The Loeb Classical Library (London: Heinemann, and Cambridge, Mass.: Harvard U.P., 1937). Vol. II, bk. III, vi-xxii, pp. 21-93.

GENERAL STUDIES OF CORNEILLE

11. Gustave Lanson, *Corneille,* Les Grands Ecrivains français (Paris: Hachette, 1898). For long the standard 'Life and Works'.

12. Valdemar Vedel, *Deux classiques français vus par un critique étranger: Corneille et son temps — Molière,* traduit du danois par Mme E. Cornet (Paris: Champion, 1935).
Brings out the background of 'baroque' taste, and Corneille's search for the 'paradoxical' in subject and character.

13. G. Couton, *Corneille,* Connaissance des Lettres, 52 (Paris: Hatier, 1958). Emphasises, perhaps too strongly, the historical background.

14. P. J. Yarrow, *Corneille* (London: Macmillan, 1963).

15. Peter France, 'Corneille', in *French Literature and its Background,* edited by John Cruickshank: 2, *The Seventeenth Century* (Oxford U. P., 1969, pp. 17-33).
Stresses the glamour, idealism, and underlying reality in Corneille's art.

16. J. H. Broome, *A Student's Guide to Corneille: four tragedies* (London: Heinemann, 1971).
Le Cid, Horace, Cinna, Polyeucte.

AMBITIOUS MODERN INTERPRETATIONS

In all this group there is a tendency to ascribe all Corneille's tragedies to a single influence (different for each critic) as if that 'explained' everything. I have expressed misgivings (p. 28 ff.) over 'explanations' derived from history or biography. The danger seems to me at least as great when they are sought in modern forms of historical or sociological theory which may be revised or discredited at any time (no. *17,* cf. p. 30) or even modern philosophical trends (no. *19*) — Corneille has so far escaped Freudian or Jungian interpretations. Nos. *18* and *19* arrive at rigid systems of interpretation which actually conflict at times with the texts they purport to elucidate.

17. Paul Bénichou, *Morales du Grand Siècle,* Bibliothèque des Idées (Paris: Gallimard, 1948), reprinted in the Collection Idées (Paris: Gallimard, 1967). The first two chapters (pp. 13-76) explain Cornelian *générosité* by an aristocratic 'feudal' mentality.

18. Octave Nadal, *Le Sentiment de l'amour dans l'œuvre de Pierre
    Corneille*, Bibliothèque des Idées (Paris: Gallimard, 1948).
    A study of keywords in Corneille (pp. 283-323) throws valuable
    light on *gloire* (cf. no. *17*) and kindred concepts; but the theory
    of the relations of love and *gloire* in Corneille visibly contradicts
    certain passages quoted (e. g. on Pauline, pp. 201 ff., cf. *Polyeucte*,
    I. 3-4).

19. Serge Doubrovsky, *Corneille et la dialectique du héros*, Biblio-
    thèque des Idées (Paris: Gallimard, 1963).
    All heroism in Corneille is explained by a neo-Hegelian formula,
    founded allegedly on an intuitive perception of a structural unity
    in the tragedies, but apparently on a monumental 'hunch' for
    which no formal proof is attempted. The interpretation rests
    on a 'projet de Maîtrise', a will to assert aristocratic superiority
    by conquest and domination. 'Meurs ou tue,' presented as the
    watchword of every Cornelian hero, is torn from a context where
    it is spoken to his son by the victim of a mortal insult, but only
    after he has made every reasonable concession to avoid a confron-
    tation (p. 92, cf. *Le Cid*, 275).

20. Jacques Maurens, *La Tragédie sans tragique: le néo-stoïcisme
    dans l'œuvre de Pierre Corneille* (Paris: Colin, 1966).
    Identifies Corneille's thought with this strand of contemporary
    philosophy.

21. André Stegmann, *L'Héroïsme cornélien: genèse et signification.
    Tome I, Corneille et la vie littéraire de son temps; tome II, L'Eu-
    rope intellectuelle et le théâtre. Signification de l'héroïsme cor-
    nélien* (Paris: Colin, 1968).
    The last section (pp. 279-651) contains a study of the plays.
    Consult table of contents.

STUDY OF "HORACE"

22. Louis Herland, *Horace, ou, Naissance de l'homme* (Paris: Editions
    de Minuit, 1952).
    See pp. 22-24, 44.

FRENCH TRAGEDY

23. Gustave Lanson, *Esquisse d'une histoire de la tragédie française*
    (New York: Columbia U. P., 1920; Paris: Champion, 1927). In
    note form. Now dated, but stimulating. Only five lines directly on
    Horace, p. 73.

24. Antoine Adam, *Histoire de la littérature française au XVIIᵉ siècle:*
    [tome I,] *l'époque d'Henri IV et de Louis XIII* (Paris: Domat,
    1948). For *Horace*, pp. 518-28.

25. Antoine Adam, *Le Théâtre classique,* Que sais-je? (Paris: P. U. F., 1970). A useful and concise survey of the whole century.

26. Jacques Truchet, *La Tragédie classique en France,* Collection SUP (Paris: P. U. F., 1975).
     Not a historical survey, but an excellent critical study.

27. Geoffrey Brereton, *Principles of Tragedy:* a rational examination of the tragic concept in life and literature (London: Routledge, 1968). A search for a definition applicable to all forms of 'tragedy'.

28. John Lough, *Seventeenth-Century French Drama: The Background* (Oxford: Clarendon Press, 1979).

ARTICLES

29. W. G. Moore, 'Corneille's *Horace* and French classical drama', *Modern Language Review,* 34, 1939, 382-95.
     Shows the play as neither a dramatized story nor a psychological study, but an impartial picture of a family facing the claims of the state.

30. Harold C. Ault, 'The Tragic Genius of Corneille', *Modern Language Review,* 45, 1950, 164-176.
     Argues that the Cornelian hero wilfully blinds himself to the claims of humanity, and remains for ever flawed.

31. D. G. Charlton, 'Corneille's Dramatic Theories and the "Didacticism" of *Horace*', *French Studies,* 15, 1961, 1-11.

32. Lawrence E. Harvey, 'Corneille's *Horace:* a study in tragic and artistic ambivalence', in *Studies in Seventeenth-Century French Literature presented to Morris Bishop,* edited by J.-J. Demorest (Ithaca, N. Y., Cornell U. P., 1962), pp. 65-97.
     Studies what I have called 'symmetries' and 'tensions' in the play.

33. A. W. H. West, *The Cornelian Hero,* University of Auckland Bulletin, No. 65, French Series No. 3 (1963).
     A comprehensive description, rather conservative, stressing will-power and self-mastery.

34. Elliott Forsyth, 'The Tragic Dilemma in *Horace*', *Australian Journal of French Studies,* 4, (1967), pp. 162-176.
     Shows that internal conflict is a favourite theme of early seventeenth-century poetry, but in tragedy is almost an innovation of Corneille.

35. R. C. Knight, '*Horace,* première tragédie classique', in *Mélanges d'histoire littéraire (XVIe-XVIIe siècle): offerts à Raymond Lebègue* (Paris: Nizet, 1969), pp. 195-200.
     Debts to tragicomedy which deeply affect subsequent French tragedy.

36. ————,'A Minimal Definition of Seventeenth-Century Tragedy', *French Studies,* 10, 1956, pp. 297-308.

'A dramatic action in which personages above the common have to react to a situation above the common, in that it involves a danger usually of death.'

37. Robert MacBride, 'Quelques Réflexions sur le héros cornélien', *XVIIᵉ siècle*, 104, 1974, pp. 45-60.
    Argues that the hero only finds himself by taking refuge in action from self-questioning caused by a crucial challenge.

38. Peter H. Nurse, 'Quelques Réflexions sur la notion du tragique dans l'œuvre de Pierre Corneille', in *Mélanges de littérature française offerts à René Pintard, Travaux de linguistique et de littérature* publiés par le Centre de Philologie et de Littératures romanes de l'Université de Strasbourg, xiii, 2 (Strasbourg: 1975), pp. 163-74.
    Argues that *Horace* may be called tragic because it points to a principle of corruption in the Roman ethos.

39. C. J. Gossip, 'Tragedy and Moral Order in Corneille's *Horace*', *Forum for Modern Language Studies*, 11, 1975, pp. 15-28.
    Reappraisal of all the personal, political, and social issues.